P O C K E T S
GEMSTONES

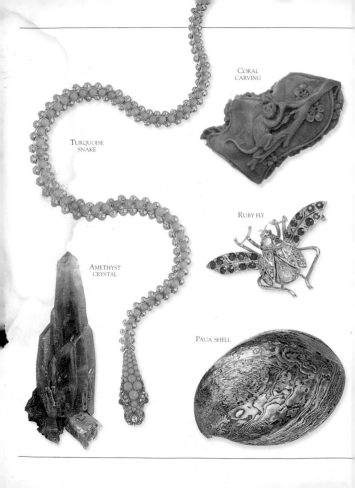

CORAL CARVING

TURQUOISE SNAKE

RUBY FLY

AMETHYST CRYSTAL

PAUA SHELL

P O C K E T S
GEMSTONES

Written by
EMMA FOA

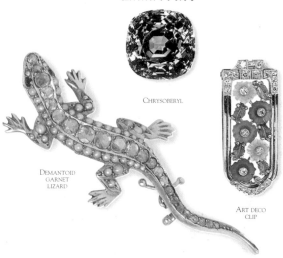

CHRYSOBERYL

DEMANTOID
GARNET
LIZARD

ART DECO
CLIP

DK PUBLISHING

LONDON, NEW YORK, TORONTO,
MELBOURNE, MUNICH, and DELHI

Project editor Joanna Buck
Designer Clair Watson
Senior editor Alastair Dougall
Senior art editors Carole Oliver, Sarah Crouch
Picture research Maureen Sheerin
Production Kate Oliver
US editor Irene Pavitt
Editorial consultants Sue Rigby, Stephen Bradshaw

REVISED EDITION
Project editor Steve Setford
Designer Sarah Crouch
Managing editor Linda Esposito
Managing art editor Jane Thomas
DTP designer Siu Yin Ho
Consultant Kim Bryan
Production Erica Rosen
US editors Margaret Parrish, Christine Heilman

Second American Edition, 2003
Published in the United States by
DK Publishing, Inc., 375 Hudson Street,
New York, New York 10014

06 07 08 10 9 8 7

Copyright © 2003 Dorling Kindersley Limited

A Cataloging-in-Publication record for the First American Edition of this book
is available from the Library of Congress.

ISBN-13: 978-0-7894-9596-9
ISBN-10: 0-7894-9596-1

Color reproduction by Colourscan, Singapore
Printed and bound in Italy by L.E.G.O.

See our complete product line at
www.dk.com

CONTENTS

How to use this book 8

INTRODUCTION TO GEMSTONES 10
The history of gemstones 12
Myth and medicine 14
What are gemstones? 16
Mining 30
Organics 32
Artificial gems 34

COLOR KEY 36
Introduction; colorless 38
Red or pink; white or silver 40
Yellow to brown 42
Green 44
Blue or violet;
black; iridescent 46

MINERAL GEMSTONES 48

Diamond 50

Ruby 54

Sapphire 56

Chrysoberyl 58

Spinel 60

Topaz 62

Emerald 64

Aquamarine 66

Zircon 68

Tourmaline 70

Garnet 72

Quartz 74

Amethyst 76

Chalcedony 78

Jade 80

Peridot 82

Moonstone 84

Opal 86

Turquoise 88

Lapis lazuli 90

Azurite and
malachite 92

ORGANIC GEMSTONES 94
Pearl 96
Coral 98
Jet 100
Ivory 102
Amber 104
Shell 106

REFERENCE SECTION 108
Legendary gems 110
Gem care 112
Making jewelry 114
Table of properties 118

Glossary 120
Resources 123
Index 124

HOW TO USE THIS BOOK

These pages show you how to use *Pockets: Gemstones*.
The book is divided into five sections. These contain
information about mineral, organic, and imitation gems,
and an easy-to-use color key. There is an introductory
section at the front, and a reference section at the back,
as well as a glossary and comprehensive index.

HEADING
The heading describes the
overall subject of the page.
This page is about emeralds.
If a subject continues over
several pages, the same
heading applies.

CAPTIONS AND ANNOTATIONS
Each illustration has an
explanatory caption. Some
also have annotations, in *italics*,
that point out the features
of an illustration.

Corner coding

Heading

Caption

Annotation

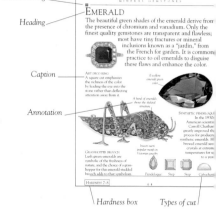

MINERAL GEMSTONES

EMERALD
The beautiful green shades of the emerald derive from
the presence of chromium and vanadium. Only the
finest quality gemstones are transparent and flawless;
most have tiny fractures or mineral
inclusions known as a "jardin," from
the French for garden. It is common
practice to oil emeralds to disguise
these flaws and enhance the color.

ART DECO RING
A square cut emphasizes
the richness of the color
by leading the eye into the
stone rather than deflecting
attention away from it.

*Excellent
emerald green
color*

*A band of emeralds
shows the deleted
structure*

SYNTHETIC PENDELOQUE
In the 1930s
American scientist
Carroll Chatham
greatly improved the
process for producing
synthetic emeralds. He
brewed emerald seed
crystals at extreme
temperatures for up
to a year

GRASSHOPPER BROOCH
Lush green emeralds are
symbolic of the freshness of
nature, and the choice of a grasshopper for the emerald-studded
brooch adds to this symbolism.

*Insects were
popular motifs in
Victorian jewelry*

Pendeloque   Step   Step   Cabochon

Hardness 7–8

8 4

Hardness box   Types of cut

CORNER CODING
The corners of the
main section pages
are color coded.

◼ COLOR KEY

◻ MINERAL
GEMSTONES

◻ ORGANIC
GEMSTONES

HARDNESS SCALE
The hardness of each gem is indicated in a box on the
bottom-left-hand corner of the main gemstone pages.
The numbers given are taken from Mohs' scale of
hardness (see pages 24–5).

RUNNING HEADS
These remind you which
section you are in. The
top of the left-hand page
gives the section name,
and the top of the right-
hand page gives the
subject heading.

LABELS
For clarity, some pictures
have labels. These
may give extra
information about
the picture, or make
identification easier.

Label

*Running
head*

ANTIQUE CABOCHON EARRINGS
These Art Deco earrings boast
large hanging emeralds. Inclusions
— marks either on or within the surface
of the stone — are clearly visible, and
the carving draws the eye toward
the surface of the gem rather
than into it.

Polished oval
cabochons are
framed in
black enamel

This gem
is larger
and lighter
in color
than the
other one

OCTAGONAL CABOCHON
Emeralds almost always have
fissures or inclusions. These may
be embedded crystals of other
materials, growth lines, or any of
a whole range of microscopic
occurrences. They tell the
story of the gem's origin
millions of years ago.

Inclusions
provide hints
to the gem's
origins

POLISHED PEBBLE
Not all emeralds have
to be prised out of rocks.
Some find their way into
river gravels, where the
action of the water tumbles
and smooths them so that
they resemble shiny pebbles.

MYTH AND MAGIC
• Hundreds of years ago,
emeralds were thought
to possess healing
powers, particularly for
restoring eyesight.
• During the
Renaissance, emeralds
were exchanged among
the aristocracy as
symbols — and tests — of
friendship, the stone
would stay intact only
if the friendship lasted.

Myth and magic box

REFERENCE SECTION
USE THE FOLLOWING step-by-step
guide to make a pair of earrings and
matching necklace. We have used
multicolored tourmalines in this
example, but you can substitute any
of different colors.
                                     size. If you want
                                     ain that you
                                     ch color.

EARRINGS

MAKING JEWELRY

1 Cut a 3in (8cm)
length of thick wire and
bend it to form a loop.

2 Make two small loops,
leaving ends slightly open.

3 Cut three 2in (5cm)
lengths of thin wire.
Make tight flat coil at
one end of piece of the
thin wire and thread
stone onto it.

4 Make small loop at other
end and twist wire round
itself to secure.

5 Trim excess wire to
avoid sharp edges. Thread
a new piece of thin wire
through existing loop, and
loop and twist wire again.

6 Thread another
gemstone onto thin
wire, make loop
and secure as
before. Repeat
steps 5 and 6 to
make V shape.

7 Secure the two stones
on the thick wire and
close up end loops with
pliers. Place completed
earring into earring wire.
Repeat whole process for
second earring.

REFERENCE SECTION
The reference section pages are tinted yellow
and appear at the back of the book. Here you
will find a chart giving each gem's physical
properties, tips for looking after jewelry, and a
stories about famous gems, and a step-by-step
guide for making a necklace and earrings set.

GEMSTONE CUTS
Symbols appear on the bottom
of the left-hand pages in the
main sections. These illustrate
the most popular cuts for each
gem (see page 29).

GLOSSARY AND INDEX
At the back of the book, there is a glossary
and an index. By referring to the index,
information on particular topics can be
found quickly. The glossary defines the
technical terms used in the book.

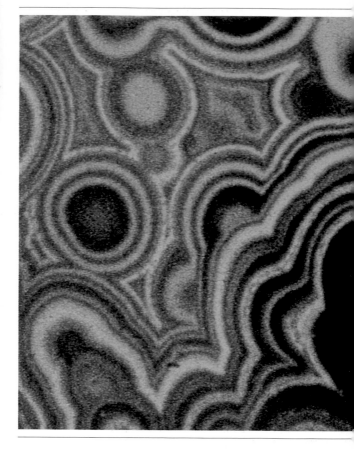

INTRODUCTION TO GEMSTONES

THE HISTORY OF GEMSTONES 12
MYTH AND MEDICINE 14
WHAT ARE GEMSTONES? 16
MINING 30
ORGANICS 32
ARTIFICIAL GEMS 34

THE HISTORY OF GEMSTONES

THE STORY OF GEMSTONES is as old as the hills in which they formed, millions of years ago. Gleaning our knowledge from ancient burial sites, we know that gems were used for weapons as well as for adornment. "Jewels," ranging from humble seashells to rough emeralds, have been found in graves dating back 20,000 years.

NECKLACE FROM THE COOK ISLANDS, OCEANIA

Local stones

In the past, people worked mainly with local gemstones. Jade was carved in China 4,500 years ago; Egyptian and Sumerian craftsmen used lapis, carnelian, and turquoise; and the Romans carved agate. In the East, diamonds, rubies, and sapphires were popular.

Beetle, symbol of rebirth

NECKLACE
Shells have always been used for adornment. This necklace dates from about CE 990 and was worn by an island chief.

WINGED SCARAB
Egyptian craftsmen combined amber, lapis lazuli, carnelian, and turquoise in this scarab beetle good-luck charm. It was found in Tutankhamun's tomb and dates to 1360 BCE.

Carved bands of black and white agate

LAPIS AND CARNELIAN NECKLACE

Cameo of owner

ROMAN BROOCH
The original owner of this beautiful brooch must have been a wealthy man. Few people could have afforded to have their portrait carved in agate and then set in gold filigree.

Amethyst bead

Etched carnelian

BEADS FOR THE NEXT LIFE
In ancient times, it was common practice for the wealthy to be buried with symbols of their status. This lapis and carnelian necklace was found in a Sumerian grave of the 1st century BCE.

TIBETAN NOMAD
Today, jewelry is an important part of many peoples' national dress. Large turquoise pebbles form the basis of this dramatic contemporary necklace from Tibet. Turquoise is a popular feature of Tibetan jewelry. It is obtained locally and is believed to have talismanic properties.

MYTH AND MEDICINE

THE BEAUTY OF GEMS, their shimmering colors and perfect forms, led people to believe that they came from the heavens. Superstitions grew up around them, and different stones were deemed able to do everything from curing drunkenness to calming the roughest seas.

MAGIC LAPIS BRACELET
This Egyptian bracelet was buried with its owner. The eye was protective.

Healing powers

The alleged power of gemstones extended beyond the supernatural – gems were thought to have medicinal properties. Chinese and Ayurvedic medicine still involves gemstones, and healing with crystals is a growing art.

GROUND LAPIS LAZULI
Powdered lapis, taken in pill form, is a regular constituent of traditional Chinese medicine. In the past, gemstones were sometimes placed on an injured part of the body.

Powdered lapis lazuli

PEARL FACE CREAM
In China, powdered pearl is prescribed for skin complaints. Pearl cream is used for the face.

CRYSTAL BALL
For centuries, balls made out of polished rock crystal have been used to "see into the future."

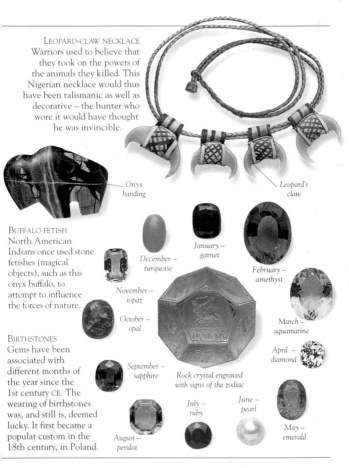

LEOPARD-CLAW NECKLACE
Warriors used to believe that they took on the powers of the animals they killed. This Nigerian necklace would thus have been talismanic as well as decorative – the hunter who wore it would have thought he was invincible.

Onyx banding

Leopard's claw

BUFFALO FETISH
North American Indians once used stone fetishes (magical objects), such as this onyx buffalo, to attempt to influence the forces of nature.

BIRTHSTONES
Gems have been associated with different months of the year since the 1st century CE. The wearing of birthstones was, and still is, deemed lucky. It first became a popular custom in the 18th century, in Poland.

December – turquoise

January – garnet

November – topaz

February – amethyst

October – opal

March – aquamarine

September – sapphire

Rock crystal engraved with signs of the zodiac

April – diamond

August – peridot

July – ruby

June – pearl

May – emerald

WHAT ARE GEMSTONES?

TO BE CONSIDERED A GEM, a substance has to be
beautiful, usually in terms of its color and the way
it reflects light. It also has to be rare and durable.
Gems are either minerals, which have a regular
internal structure and fixed chemical
composition, or organics, which
are produced by plants and animals.

Ruby crystal

NATURAL CRYSTAL
Ruby crystals form in igneous
and metamorphic rocks. They
are sometimes washed out of
these rocks into
river gravels.

MINERAL GEMS
The majority
of gems, like the
ruby shown here,
are minerals that
crystallize within
the Earth's crust.
Ruby forms at high
temperatures and pressures
and is brought to the Earth's
surface by rising magma or by
prolonged erosion.

CUT STONES
Rubies are
second only
to diamonds
in terms of
hardness. They
are prized for the richness of their
color and their rarity. Rubies are
one of the most expensive gems.

CABOCHON CUT
Before deciding on a cut,
the gemstone cutter
will inspect
the crystal.
Cutting as
a cabochon
reveals a star
effect when certain
markings are present.

Star-effect ruby

SYNTHETIC GEMS
Synthetic gems are created in laboratories and have chemical properties similar to those of real gemstones. This synthetic ruby was manufactured by the Verneuil method (see page 34).

Synthetic ruby

Crystals growing

FLUX-MELT TECHNIQUE
French chemist Edmond Frémy discovered a method for growing ruby crystals by melting aluminum oxide and chromium in a crucible.

Ruby crystals in matrix

ORGANICS
Organic gems are produced by living organisms. This group includes jet, pearl, coral, amber, ivory, and shell. Organics are softer than mineral gems and usually opaque. They tend to be carved and polished rather than faceted (cut).

Oyster shell

Pearl bead

Round, faceted ruby

JEWELRY
Gemstones are generally faceted and mounted so that light can shine through. This ruby and diamond cluster brooch dates from about 1915.

RUBY AND DIAMOND BROOCH

PEARL IN OYSTER SHELL

World map

Deposits of gemstones have been found in virtually every part of the world. They are dependent on particular geological conditions, which is why some stones are much rarer than others.

DIAMONDS
Wind, water, and erosion can transport gems to new locations. Here, an Indonesian man pans for diamonds.

UNITED STATES

Atlantic Ocean

COLOMBIA

BRAZIL

KEY TO SYMBOLS

DIAMOND	RUBY	SAPPHIRE	EMERALD
AQUAMARINE	CHRYSOBERYL	TOPAZ	TOURMALINE
PERIDOT	GARNET	PEARL	OPAL

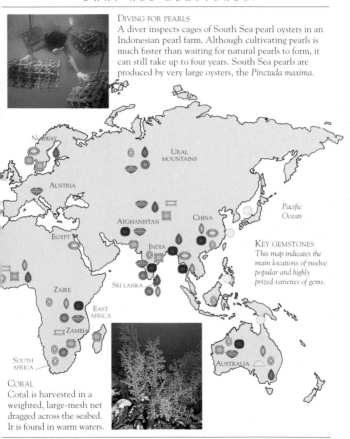

DIVING FOR PEARLS
A diver inspects cages of South Sea pearl oysters in an Indonesian pearl farm. Although cultivating pearls is much faster than waiting for natural pearls to form, it can still take up to four years. South Sea pearls are produced by very large oysters, the *Pinctada maxima*.

NORWAY

URAL MOUNTAINS

AUSTRIA

Pacific Ocean

AFGHANISTAN   CHINA

EGYPT

INDIA

KEY GEMSTONES
This map indicates the main locations of twelve popular and highly prized varieties of gems.

ZAIRE

SRI LANKA

EAST AFRICA

ZAMBIA

SOUTH AFRICA

AUSTRALIA

CORAL
Coral is harvested in a weighted, large-mesh net dragged across the seabed. It is found in warm waters.

How gemstones are formed

Mineral gemstones are formed within the Earth as a result of certain physical and chemical conditions. Heat and pressure are the main external factors involved in gemstone formation. Some are brought to the surface by volcanic eruptions; others are found in rocks or in gem gravels – the deposits left by rivers and streams as they gradually erode rocks.

1 Diamond and pyrope garnet crystallize at high pressures in the Earth's mantle.

2 High pressures in the Earth's crust can lead to the formation of jadeite.

3 Peridot occurs in basaltic and ultrabasic rocks.

4 Chrysoberyl, topaz, aquamarine, tourmaline, quartz, spessartine, and moonstone crystallize when coarse-grained igneous granites (pegmatites) cool down.

5 Emeralds occur when granitic fluids come into contact with rocks containing chromium.

6 Extreme pressure and temperature changes in shale can give rise to the crystallization of ruby, sapphire, chrysoberyl, spinel, and garnet.

GRANITE

Peridot forms deep beneath the Earth's surface

PERIDOT

MALACHITE

Malachite often occurs in rounded masses

7 Ruby, sapphire, spinel, zircon, lapis lazuli, spessartine, and grossular garnet form when hot granitic fluids react with impure shales and limestones.

CROSS SECTION OF EARTH

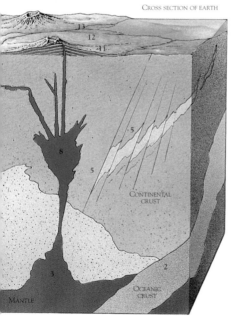

13
12
11

5

5

8

5

CONTINENTAL CRUST

2

3

MANTLE

OCEANIC CRUST

8 Rising magma carries gem minerals to the Earth's surface, where they are trapped in basalt lavas.

9 Turquoise, malachite, and azurite tend to form close to the Earth's surface, where ore bodies come into contact with water.

10 Opal is found in porous sedimentary rocks and sometimes in cavities in volcanic rocks. It forms during cooling of silica-rich groundwater.

Layer of precious opal

OPAL

11 Silica-rich liquids deposit citrine, amethyst, agate, and opal in gas cavities in lavas.

12 Various weathering processes break down gem-bearing rocks.

13 Gems are washed into river gravels.

Crystal structure

Most gemstones are composed of crystals, which grow in a regular, three-dimensional pattern. Crystals are classified into seven different systems, according to the symmetry of their faces, or flat surfaces. The overall shape formed by the surfaces is called the "habit." Some gemstones have an irregular shape, known as "amorphous."

CHRYSOPRASE

TOPAZ

REGULAR STRUCTURE
As with the other members of the chalcedony family, chrysoprase has a trigonal structure (see facing page), which is characterized by a threefold symmetry.

JET

Fine-grained, rough surface

AMORPHOUS
Jet, along with amber and ivory, is an organic gem that does not fall within the seven crystal systems. Instead, its structure is amorphous, which means literally "without form."

Line of cleavage

CLEAVAGE
The way in which a stone breaks, or cleaves, depends on its planes of weakness. These planes relate to its crystal structure and are usually parallel, perpendicular, or diagonal to the crystal faces.

CRYSTAL STRUCTURE

AXES OF SYMMETRY

Each crystal system has different axes of symmetry – imaginary lines around which the crystal rotates and still shows the same aspect. The diagrams indicate the minimum number of times a crystal shows the same aspect in each rotation.

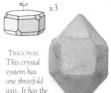

SPINEL

TRIGONAL
This crystal system has one threefold axis. It has the same axes of symmetry as the hexagonal.

MILKY QUARTZ

CUBIC
Spinel is a typical cubic crystal. The cubic system has the highest symmetry – three fourfold axes.

TETRAGONAL
This system is defined by one fourfold axis. The zircon (right) displays double pyramidal ends.

ZIRCON

MONOCLINIC
Gems such as azurite, moonstone, and jade belong to the monoclinic system, which has one two-fold axis.

AZURITE

HEXAGONAL
Emerald and aquamarine belong to this system. They have one sixfold axis of symmetry.

AQUAMARINE

ORTHORHOMBIC
There are a minimum of three twofold axes in this system.

TOPAZ

TRICLINIC
Triclinic gems are unusual in that they have no axes of symmetry and are therefore the least symmetrical.

TURQUOISE

Physical properties

Mineral gemstones can be identified and classified according to certain properties, ranging from their relative hardness to their relative weights. Hardness is measured on a scale of 1 to 10, with diamond being 10. Specific gravity reflects the density of a gem, and carats are used to measure its weight.

AGATE

ROCK CRYSTAL

Treelike inclusion

MOHS' HARDNESS SCALE

The German mineralogist Friedrich Mohs devised a scale as a means of classifying the relative hardness of minerals. Hardness was defined as the ability to scratch another mineral, so that each mineral on his scale can scratch those below it and be scratched by those above it.

INCLUSIONS

Internal features of gems such as trapped solids, liquids, or gases are called inclusions. These can be invaluable in identifying certain gems. Needle-like inclusions are often present in rock crystal, and "landscape" features tend to form in agates, due to iron oxides and hydroxides.

1
TALC

2
GYPSUM

3
CALCITE

4
FLUORITE

5
APATITE

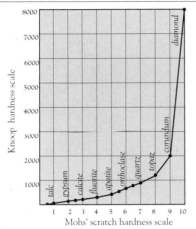

SPECIFIC GRAVITY

The density of a gem is called its specific gravity (SG). It is calculated by comparing a stone's weight with the weight of an equal amount of water. The SG of aquamarine, for example, is 2.69, which means it is 2.69 times heavier than an equal amount of water.

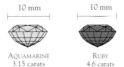

AQUAMARINE
3.15 carats

RUBY
4.6 carats

Ruby has a much higher SG, at 4.00. Consequently, a 0.4-in (10-mm) brilliant-cut ruby will weigh 4.6 carats, compared to an aquamarine's 3.15 carats. One carat equals one-fifth of a gram. The word "carat" derives from the carob seed – a standard for weighing gems for centuries.

THE KNOOP HARDNESS SCALE

The intervals between the numbers on Mohs' scale do not represent equal increases in hardness – for example, diamond is four times harder than corundum, but is next to it on the scale. Knoop's scale, instead, reveals the varying degrees of hardness of Mohs' ten minerals.

MOHS' MINERALS

6
ORTHOCLASE

7
QUARTZ

8
TOPAZ

9
CORUNDUM

10
DIAMOND

Color and luster

A gemstone's value depends largely on its color and the way in which it reflects light. The term "luster" describes the amount of light reflected from the surface of a mineral; gems range from highly lustrous (adamantine) to waxy (low luster). Their color depends on how they absorb light, as well as the type and amount of impurities they contain. Some gems occur in only one color – for example, malachite, which is always green.

SPLITTING LIGHT
White light is made up of all the colors of the rainbow. If a gem appears red, it is because red is reflected back, while the other colors are absorbed.

IDENTIFYING GEMSTONES
Many gems are so similar in color that it is impossible to tell them apart with the naked eye. Gemologists use an instrument known as a spectroscope, which separates light into its spectrum of colors. This reveals the way each stone absorbs bands of colored light. The pattern that each gemstone makes is like its individual "fingerprint."

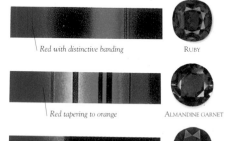

Red with distinctive banding

RUBY

Red tapering to orange

ALMANDINE GARNET

ABSORPTION SPECTRA *Broad band of black*

GLASS

PARTICOLORED GEMS

Some gemstones are of two or more colors. Tourmalines are excellent examples of this, since a single crystal may display as many as 15 different colors or shades. This watermelon tourmaline has three bands of color.

Lapis with white flecks of calcite

WATERMELON TOURMALINE

IDIOCHROMATIC GEMS

Although the shade may vary, lapis lazuli is always blue. This is due to its sulfur content, which is an essential part of its composition. Gems of this type are known as "idiochromatic," or self-colored.

Vitreous luster

Resinous luster

ADAMANTINE LUSTER

Diamonds typically have an "adamantine" luster, which is the highest and most desirable degree of sheen. The brilliant cut is popular for diamonds since it maximizes this effect.

VITREOUS LUSTER

Malachite has a glasslike quality, known as a vitreous luster. It is also opaque – it lets no light through. The characteristic green color of malachite is caused by its copper content.

RESINOUS LUSTER

This polished amber bead has a resinous sheen. Amber with less shine than this is often called "waxy."

Adamantine luster

Cut and polish

Uncut gems often look like ordinary stones. It is the cutting and polishing processes that transform "rocks" into jewels. Gems may be cut into a number of flat surfaces, known as facets, or rounded and polished into cabochons.

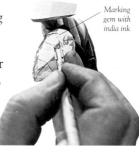

Marking gem with india ink

1 ROUGH
Model of the rough crystal ready for faceting.

Crown

Girdle

Girdle

Pavilion

2 GRIND
The top of the crystal is sawn off, and the stone is rounded using a diamond grinder.

FACETING A GEMSTONE
Decisions on the best style of cut are reached by careful examination of a gem's form and structure. The final gem may be as little as 40 percent of the original.

Crown facets

3 CUT
The main facets are added to the crown.

Star facet

5 FINAL CUT
The standard round brilliant cut has 58 facets, precisely angled and in perfect proportion to one another.

Crown facet

4 TOP AND BOTTOM
The eight main crown facets are completed, and facets are added below the girdle.

REFLECTING LIGHT

The ideal cut maximizes the amount of light that is reflected back from the stone. If a gem cut is too deep or too shallow, the stone will not sparkle.

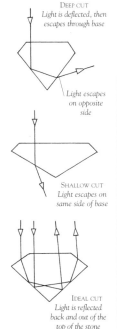

DEEP CUT
Light is deflected, then escapes through base

Light escapes on opposite side

SHALLOW CUT
Light escapes on same side of base

IDEAL CUT
Light is reflected back and out of the top of the stone

HI-TECH CUTTING

Computers have revolutionized the cutting and polishing processes. This operator oversees the faceting operation on screen.

PRECISION CUTTING

TYPES OF CUT

This table shows the most popular cuts, which are shown for each of the main gemstones featured in this book. Faceted cuts are grouped as brilliant, mixed, step, and fancy. Nonfaceted gems are also listed.

BRILLIANT CUTS	Round	Oval			
MIXED CUTS	Mixed	Cushion			
STEP CUTS	Octagonal	Oval	Baguette	Table	Square
FANCY CUTS	Pendeloque	Marquise			
POLISHED/ CAMEO CUTS	Cabochon	Bead	Cameo	Polished	

MINING

THE COLLECTING OF GEMS can be as simple as panning for stones in a riverbed, or involve vastly expensive, technologically advanced mining equipment. In some parts of the world, traditional methods are the most cost-effective, but for stones such as diamonds, which are often embedded deep in volcanic rocks, the most modern mining processes have to be used.

PANNING FOR RUBIES
Thai workers pan for rubies using an age-old method. The hardness and weight of rubies allow them to be sifted from river gravel and then picked out by hand.

PANNING FOR RUBIES IN THAILAND

OPAL MINING IN AUSTRALIA
Opal is often found in sandstone and so can be dislodged relatively easily. Electronic diggers are used underground, and gem-bearing rubble is then sucked up to the surface, where it is sorted.

MATRIX OPAL
Opal is a silica gel containing a high proportion of water. It forms by filling cavities in a rock and hardening.

Hardened sandy clay

GEM TREASURE TROVE

Panning operates on the principle that lighter materials are washed away by the swirling action of water, leaving behind precious minerals. This technique is often used in areas such as Myanmar (Burma).

SOUTH AFRICAN DIAMOND MINE
The scale of a diamond-mining operation is astounding, in terms of both the size of the pit and the amount of equipment needed. Over 250 tons of rock have to be blasted for every finished diamond carat – for each 0.007 oz (0.2 g)!

Precious stones mixed in with other minerals

TRAWLING FOR DIAMONDS
The seabed off the Namibian coast is an important source of diamonds. The latest recovery technique involves large, offshore ships that pump gravel containing diamonds up to the surface.

ORGANICS

GEMS THAT ARE THE PRODUCTS of plants and animals, rather than having a mineral origin, are known as organics. Pearls, coral, and amber come into this category, as do ivory, jet, and different types of shell. These materials have been prized and used as ornaments for thousands of years.

JAPANESE PEARL DIVER

CORAL
Coral grows in warm waters at depths of 10–1,000 ft (3–300 m). Its tree-like branches tend to be dull and grainy when harvested, but can be polished to a high luster.

CORAL BEAD

FISHING FOR PEARLS
Japan pioneered the development of cultured pearls at the turn of the 20th century, and it now dominates the world pearl market. Here a diver swims with a large bucket to gather specially farmed *akoya* oysters, with their valuable pearls.

Pearl in oyster

CORAL REEF

FOSSILIZED JEWEL
Organic gems are softer than mineral gemstones and tend to be less durable. Jet is 2.5 on Mohs' scale of hardness, the same as a fingernail. It is fossilized wood, a product of trees that lived millions of years ago, and has been used decoratively since the Bronze Age.

FOSSILIZED WOOD

JET BEAD

IVORY

Elephants' tusks have long been the main source of ivory, but are by no means the only one. The teeth and tusks of many other mammals also contain ivory and are now often used in preference to elephant ivory, since elephants are a protected species. Ivory is prized for its color, ease of carving, and durability.

CARVED IVORY

Elephant tusks

AMBER

Like jet, amber is a fossil derived from trees, but in this case from the resin rather than the compacted remains of the wood. It is characteristically a golden orange color, and this, coupled with its translucence and resinous luster, have made it popular for jewelry.

Fossilized resin from pine tree

TORTOISESHELL

The term "tortoiseshell" is confusing, since it refers to the carapace (upper shell) of a hawksbill turtle rather than that of a tortoise. It was extremely popular for hair ornaments and small boxes in the early part of the 20th century, but it is now a protected substance.

TORTOISESHELL

HAWKSBILL TURTLE

Resinous luster

AMBER BEAD

Turtle with tortoiseshell carapace

ARTIFICIAL GEMS

THE DEMAND FOR RARE GEMSTONES has led
to the production of countless imitations,
some more successful than others. These
copies fall into three categories: gems that
look like the real thing, but have a different
composition; synthetic gems, which are made
in laboratories and are almost exact copies of
natural gems; and composite stones, which
consist of several parts cemented together.

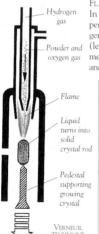

Hydrogen gas

Powder and oxygen gas

Flame

Liquid turns into solid crystal rod

Pedestal supporting growing crystal

VERNEUIL TECHNIQUE

FLAME-FUSION TECHNIQUE
In 1891, the French scientist August Verneuil
perfected a technique for producing synthetic
gems. He sifted powdered crystals into a flame
(left), and melted them onto a holder. The
melted crystal was then removed from the heat,
and it formed a solid crystal (right, top section).

FLAME FUSION

GROWING CRYSTALS
Many crystals grow in hot fluids as they cool down.
Although this process can be replicated in a
laboratory, it takes many years to produce gem-quality
crystals in this way, and so is not commercially viable.

STUBBY CRYSTALS START TO FORM

CRYSTALS BEGIN TO TAKE SHAPE

SYNTHETIC EMERALD
This pendeloque-cut emerald has been made by the flux-melt technique (see page 17). Its composition and structure are the same as that of a natural emerald.

Synthetic emerald

COMPOSITE STONE

Red garnet on top of green glass

IDENTIFYING GEMS
It is usually possible to distinguish between real and artificial gems with a small hand lens, called a loupe. This one has tenfold magnification.

HAND-HELD LENS

GARNET-TOPPED EMERALD DOUBLET
This composite stone is made of a red garnet top and a green glass base. It appears green despite the garnet and is intended to pass for an emerald. The garnet-topped doublet is a common composite stone.

GILSON OPAL

OPAL
The French manufacturer Pierre Gilson has imitated the opal's iridescence. However, these opals have patches of color and are not perfect replicas.

Simulated rubies, probably glass

IMITATION RUBY AND DIAMOND PENDANT

FABULOUS FAKE
This pendant is made of simulated rubies and diamonds, probably glass. The gems are imitation rather than synthetic, as they do not have the same chemical composition as real stones.

Fake diamonds

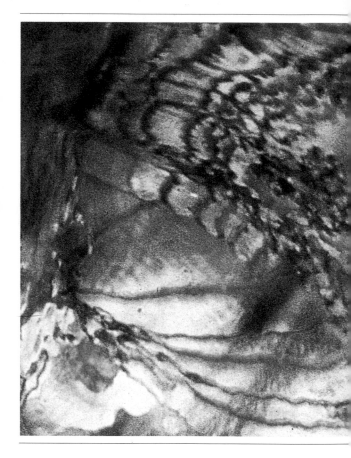

COLOR KEY

INTRODUCTION; COLORLESS 38
RED OR PINK; WHITE OR SILVER 40
YELLOW TO BROWN 42
GREEN 44
BLUE OR VIOLET;
BLACK; IRIDESCENT 46

INTRODUCTION

THE MAJORITY OF GEMS are colored by metallic elements, notably chromium, iron, manganese, titanium, and copper. Depending on the type and amount of metal contained in a gemstone, its color can vary greatly. In this section, gemstones are categorized according to seven basic color bands.

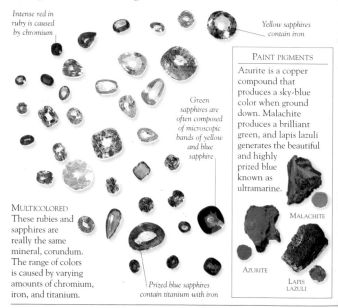

Intense red in ruby is caused by chromium

Yellow sapphires contain iron

Green sapphires are often composed of microscopic bands of yellow and blue sapphire

MULTICOLORED
These rubies and sapphires are really the same mineral, corundum. The range of colors is caused by varying amounts of chromium, iron, and titanium.

Prized blue sapphires contain titanium with iron

PAINT PIGMENTS

Azurite is a copper compound that produces a sky-blue color when ground down. Malachite produces a brilliant green, and lapis lazuli generates the beautiful and highly prized blue known as ultramarine.

MALACHITE

AZURITE

LAPIS LAZULI

COLORLESS

ALWAYS COLORLESS

ROCK CRYSTAL
(*Quartz pp. 74–5*)

ACHROITE
(*Tourmaline pp. 70–1*)

IMITATION
DIAMONDS
Cubic zirconia
Strontium titanate
Glass

USUALLY COLORLESS

DIAMOND
(*pp. 50–3*)

OTHER GEMS
Scheelite
Celestine
Danburite
Cerussite

ORTHOCLASE
(*Moonstone family pp. 84–5*)

SOMETIMES COLORLESS

ZIRCON
(*pp. 68–9*)

MOONSTONE
(*pp. 84–5*)

SAPPHIRE
(*pp. 56–7*)

RED OR PINK

ALWAYS RED OR PINK

PINK GROSSULAR
(Garnet pp. 72–3)

RUBY
(pp. 54–5)

ALMANDINE
(Garnet pp. 72–3)

PYROPE
(Garnet pp. 72–3)

RUBELLITE
(Tourmaline pp. 70–1)

USUALLY RED OR PINK

SPESSARTINE
(Garnet pp. 72–3)

SOMETIMES RED OR PINK

TOPAZ
(pp. 62–3)

WATERMELON TOURMALINE
(pp. 70–1)

SAPPHIRE
(pp. 56–7)

CORAL
(*pp. 98–9*)

SPINEL
(*pp. 60–1*)

JADEITE
(*Jade pp. 80–1*)

WHITE OR SILVER

ALWAYS WHITE OR SILVER

IVORY
(*pp. 102–3*)

DONKEY'S-EAR ABALONE
(*Shell pp. 106–7*)

MILKY QUARTZ
(*pp. 74–5*)

USUALLY WHITE OR SILVER

PEARL
(*pp. 96–7*)

SHELL
(*pp. 106–7*)

SOMETIMES WHITE OR SILVER

NEPHRITE
(*Jade pp. 80–1*)

YELLOW–BROWN

ALWAYS YELLOW–BROWN

PADPARADSCHA
(Sapphire pp. 56–7)

CARNELIAN
(Chalcedony pp. 78–9)

FIRE OPAL
(pp. 86–7)

SARDONYX
(Chalcedony pp. 78–9)

HESSONITE
(Garnet pp. 72–3)

DRAVITE
(Tourmaline pp. 70–1)

TORTOISESHELL
(Shell pp. 106–7)

CITRINE
(Quartz pp. 74–5)

OTHER GEMS
Heliodor
Sunstone
Cassiterite
Smoky quartz

USUALLY YELLOW–BROWN

ORTHOCLASE
(*Moonstone family pp. 84–5*)

AMBER
(*pp. 104–5*)

OTHER GEMS
Vesuvianite
Titanite
Axinite
Staurolite

SOMETIMES YELLOW–BROWN

SPESSARTINE
(*Garnet pp. 72–3*)

CHRYSOBERYL
(*pp. 58–9*)

CHATOYANT QUARTZ
(*Chalcedony pp. 78–9*)

MOSS AGATE
(*Chalcedony pp. 78–9*)

CAT'S EYE
(*Chalcedony pp. 78–9*)

SAPPHIRE
(*pp. 56–7*)

GREEN

ALWAYS GREEN

EMERALD
(pp. 64–5)

PERIDOT
(pp. 82–3)

BLOODSTONE
(Chalcedony pp. 78–9)

UVAROVITE
(Garnet pp. 72–3)

CHRYSOPRASE
(Chalcedony pp. 78–9)

MALACHITE
(pp. 92–3)

USUALLY GREEN

JADEITE
(Jade pp. 80–1)

NEPHRITE
(Jade pp. 80–1)

DEMANTOID
(Garnet pp. 72–3)

SOMETIMES GREEN

AGATE
(*Chalcedony pp. 78–9*)

SAPPHIRE
(*pp. 56–7*)

WATERMELON TOURMALINE
(*pp. 70–1*)

DIAMOND
(*pp. 50–1*)

OTHER GEMS
Paua Shell
Fluorite
Smithsonite
Euclase
Kyanite

ZIRCON
(*pp. 68–9*)

GROSSULAR GARNET
(*Garnet pp. 72–3*)

GARNET-TOPPED DOUBLET
(*pp. 72–3*)

TOURMALINE
(*pp. 70–1*)

BLUE OR VIOLET

ALWAYS BLUE OR VIOLET

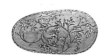

AQUAMARINE
(pp. 66–7)

TURQUOISE
(pp. 88–9)

AZURITE
(pp. 92–3)

LAPIS LAZULI
(pp. 90–1)

AMETHYST
(pp. 76–7)

HAUYNE
(Lapis lazuli pp. 90–1)

SOMETIMES BLUE OR VIOLET

TOPAZ
(pp. 62–3)

SAPPHIRE
(pp. 56–7)

SPINEL
(pp. 60–1)

BLACK

ALWAYS BLACK

JET
(pp. 100–1)

SCHORL
(Tourmaline pp. 70–1)

ARTIFICIAL JET
Cannel coal
Vulcanized
rubber
Glass

SOMETIMES BLACK

CORAL
(pp. 98–9)

DIAMOND
(pp. 50–1)

PEARL
(pp. 96–7)

IRIDESCENT

OPAL
(pp. 86–7)

FIRE AGATE
(Chalcedony pp. 78–9)

MOTHER-OF-PEARL
(Shell pp. 106–7)

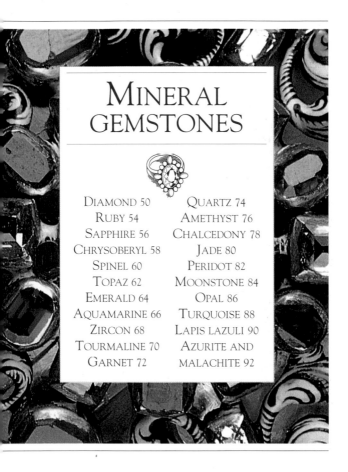

MINERAL GEMSTONES

DIAMOND 50
RUBY 54
SAPPHIRE 56
CHRYSOBERYL 58
SPINEL 60
TOPAZ 62
EMERALD 64
AQUAMARINE 66
ZIRCON 68
TOURMALINE 70
GARNET 72

QUARTZ 74
AMETHYST 76
CHALCEDONY 78
JADE 80
PERIDOT 82
MOONSTONE 84
OPAL 86
TURQUOISE 88
LAPIS LAZULI 90
AZURITE AND
MALACHITE 92

DIAMOND

KNOWN AS THE "king of gems," the diamond is the most precious of gemstones, famed both for its fiery brilliance and for being the hardest mineral on Earth. Its name derives from the Greek word *adamas*, which means "invincible." Diamonds are a form of carbon. They occur in a range of colors, the most popular being colorless.

DIAMOND IN MATRIX
Diamonds are sometimes found in conglomerate rock, as shown here. It is a solidified mixture of pebbles and grains.

MYTH AND MAGIC
• Hindus believed that a flawed diamond would bring misfortune.
• The Greeks thought that diamonds could protect against poisons.
• In medieval times, those who could afford to wore a diamond jewel to safeguard against the plague.

PENDANT

PEARL AND DIAMOND PENDANT
In the Victorian era, sporting diamond jewelry was one of the favorite ways of displaying wealth. This piece dates from the 1850s.

Diamond weighs 2.48 carats

ENGAGEMENT RING
Diamonds, symbols of love and fidelity, have been used in engagement rings since the 15th century.

Brilliant   Cushion   Pendeloque

DIAMOND NECKLACE

This necklace containing diamond loops and festoons dates from about 1870. The diamonds are brilliants of varying sizes.

NECKLACE

Brilliant cut is typical for diamonds

COLORED DIAMONDS

These gem-quality, colored stones are called fancies and fetch a very high price. Traces of nitrogen give brown, yellow, green, and black stones their color; boron is present in blue diamonds.

Champagne

Black

Silver

Green

Purple

Rose

Gold

FANCIES

BUTTERFLY BROOCH

Brilliant-cut diamonds

DIAMOND BRACELET

Flexible links

BUTTERFLY

Dating from about 1850, this delicate openwork brooch consists of over 125 brilliant-cut diamonds. The ruby eyes form a striking contrast to the shimmering white wings.

BRACELET

Designed with flexible-band links, this diamond-studded bracelet dates from the late 19th century.

Famous diamonds

The history of diamonds is one of untold greed, intrigue, and deceit. Countries have been plundered for them, wars fought, and beautiful women lost and won. However, not all diamonds have brought about such destruction. The Taylor–Burton diamond, for example, was used to save lives: in 1978, it was sold to finance a hospital in Botswana.

TAYLOR–BURTON
The actor Richard Burton bought this pear-shaped diamond for his wife Elizabeth Taylor in 1969. Nine years later they divorced, and she put it up for auction.

Gem cut from a rough stone of 241 carats

DRESDEN GREEN
Known as the Dresden Green, this is the largest green diamond in existence, measuring roughly 30 x 20 x 10 mm and weighing 41 carats.

CULLINAM I
Also known as the Great Star of Africa, this stone was found in South Africa's Premier Mine in 1905. It took three polishers, working 14 hours a day, eight months to cut and polish it! Presented to King Edward VII in 1908, it is now set in the British Imperial Scepter.

THE TIFFANY
This diamond was bought by Tiffany's, the New York jeweler, in 1879 for $18,000. Just over 100 years later, it was valued at $12 million.

Largest known yellow diamond

THE SANCY
In the 16th century, the Sancy was used to finance a war in Europe. The servant bearing it swallowed the stone when attacked. The stone was later retrieved from his stomach!

THE HOPE
Despite its name, owners of the Hope Diamond are said to be cursed. One was eaten by wild beasts; Louis XVI of France was guillotined; a Dutch jeweler committed suicide; an actress was shot on stage while wearing it; and her lover, whose gift it was, was stabbed to death!

KOH-I-NOOR
The Koh-i-noor passed rapidly from owner to owner – Indian, Moghul, and Persian. It was presented to Queen Victoria in 1850 and was set in the crown worn by the Queen Mother in 1937.

Koh-i-noor Diamond set in Maltese cross

RUBY

THE CLASSIC RUBY is a deep, rich red, although the stone can appear in shades from pink to purple to brown, depending on the chemical content. Rubies are second only to diamonds in terms of hardness, which, along with the vibrancy of their color, makes them highly prized for jewelry. Like sapphires, they are a form of corundum, and the finest stones come from Myanmar (Burma).

Five rubies hang within a diamond border

A typical cut for rubies

CUSHION MIXED CUT
Mixed-cut stones usually have a rounded outline, with the upper section cut as brilliants and the lower section step cut. Rubies are usually cut this way.

GEORGIAN DROPS
Diamonds are often used to set off the color of the ruby, as in these earrings from around 1800.

Brilliant   Step   Cabochon   Mixed

HARDNESS 9

EDWARDIAN PENDANT
The pale tones of this ruby suggest that it was mined in Sri Lanka. Hindus considered light-colored rubies "female" gems, and the darker ones, "male."

FLORAL SPRAY
This brooch is set with circular rubies, step-cut diamonds, and a large brilliant-cut diamond in the center.

Deep red mixed-cut rubies

Pale ruby cut as a cabochon

RUBY PENDANT

CLASSIC RING
Traditionally given as a 40th-wedding-anniversary present, the ruby is also the gemstone of those born in July.

MYTH AND MAGIC
- At the time of the Borgias (15th–16th centuries), rubies were thought to counteract poison – and so were much in demand!

- Rubbed on the skin, these gemstones were once thought to restore youth and vitality.

- In the Middle Ages, the ruby was viewed as a stone of prophecy. People believed it would darken when its wearer was in danger.

Six-rayed star

STAR RUBY
The color of this cabochon is known as "pigeon's-blood red" – pure red with a hint of blue – and is the most sought after shade.

SAPPHIRE

THESE STONES come in a range of yellows, pinks, and greens, as well as the better-known blue variety. The deep blue "heavenly" sapphires were, and to some extent still are, deemed holy: popes, cardinals, and bishops have worn them since the Middle Ages. They are known as the jewels of chastity.

Diamonds

SHIMMERING BROOCH
In its purest form the sapphire is colorless; traces of vanadium render it violet. Here the clarity of the diamonds enhances the tones of the central sapphire.

RING
The unusual color of this sapphire ring is due to the presence of a small amount of iron.

MYTH AND MAGIC
• At one time, sapphires were thought to exude heavenly rays that had the power to kill all poisonous creatures.
• The Persians thought the Earth rested on a giant sapphire and that the blue of the heavens was its reflection.

GREEN CUSHION CUT
Sapphires that come from Australia and Montana are often of a dark green hue.

Brilliant Cabochon Cameo Brilliant Cushion

HARDNESS 9

LATE VICTORIAN NECKLACE
The stones in this intricate necklace are of a pale blue variety. Blue sapphires derive their color from mixtures of iron and traces of titanium, while green varieties are due to greater quantities of iron, and pink to the presence of chromium.

Diamond quatrefoils form links

Brilliant-cut sapphire

The sapphire and diamond drop is detachable

STAR CABOCHON
Star sapphires were considered the most potent of amulets. The three intersecting lines that form the star's "rays" represented faith, hope, and destiny.

SAPPHIRE EARRINGS
These delicate sapphire and diamond drop earrings date from about 1890. The cabochons are of highly prized cornflower blue and probably come from Sri Lanka.

Diamond-set leaves

Cabochon cut

OVAL MIXED CUT
Like rubies, pink sapphires are thought to ward off ill-health and misfortune, particularly when worn on the skin.

CHRYSOBERYL

THE NAME "CHRYSOBERYL" comes from the stone's beryllium content plus the Greek *chrysos*, meaning "golden." Interesting types are alexandrite, which can change from green to red, mauve, or brown, depending on the light, and cat's-eye, which looks as it sounds and allegedly protects against the "evil eye."

Characteristic wedge-shaped ends

CRYSTALS
The best chrysoberyl has been found in the Ural Mountains of western Russia. Other rich sources are Sri Lanka, Zimbabwe, Tanzania, and Brazil.

Gold filigree setting

BROOCH
At 8.5 on Mohs' scale, chrysoberyl is one of the hardest stones and so is particularly prized for jewelry. This Victorian piece is made of over 20 individual mixed-cut stones.

Mixed-cut gems

CUSHION MIXED CUT
Here hundreds of facets reflect the golden color for which chrysoberyl is renowned. Despite the stone's brilliance, it is thought to lack "fire."

Brilliant   Cushion   Cabochon   Mixed

HARDNESS 8.5

ALEXANDRITE
Discovered in 1830 in the emerald mines of the Urals, this variety of chrysoberyl was named in honor of Czar Alexander II. The stone changes from green to light red in artificial light.

NECKLACE
This early-19th-century necklace consists of pale, honey-colored chrysoberyls in a cannetille setting – an embroidery term for gold thread with a spiral twist.

SPANISH DESIGN
The chrysoberyl in this 18th-century ring was collected from a vein running through chalk. The pale yellow stones are a classic cushion cut, and the large oval ring is probably of Spanish or Portuguese origin.

Filigree work in palmette motif

Pale yellow stones

Near-white line across the center

ART DECO RING
Cat's-eye chrysoberyl is also known as cymophane. It is always cut as a cabochon, and its value increases in proportion to the narrowness and intensity of its flash of light.

CAT'S-EYE

MYTH
AND MAGIC
• In the East, cat's-eyes are used to ward off evil spirits. In the West, they are used in crystal healing.

• Cat's eyes are also used medicinally in India, particularly as a remedy for cancer.

SPINEL

THE COLOR VARIATIONS of spinel – blue, yellow, and red – are caused by various metallic impurities. The most popular spinel is a ruby red, which contains chromiun and iron. Many treasures of state throughout the world sport massive red spinels, mistaken for rubies. The British Imperial State Crown is no exception.

Diamond surround

DROP EARRINGS
Large pendeloque-cut spinels hang from diamond frames. These earrings form part of an 18th-century jewelry set, which includes a tiara, necklace, and hair ornament.

OCTAGONAL STEP CUT
This pink spinel comes from Myanmar (Burma), a rich source of river gravel deposits.

| Cushion | Mixed | Step | Brilliant |

HARDNESS 8

BRITISH CROWN

The Black Prince's Ruby is the spinel in the center of the British Imperial State Crown. It was a gift from Pedro the Cruel, king of Spain, to the Black Prince, son of Edward III of England, in 1367 for his help in battle.

BRITISH IMPERIAL STATE CROWN

OVAL BRILLIANT CUT

Pure spinel is colorless. This stone has a pinkish mauve tinge due to small amounts of impurities. Liquid-filled inclusions are visible.

MIXED-CUT RED SPINEL

Until the 19th century, red spinels were known as Balas rubies, possibly named after their source, Balascia, now Badakhshan, in Afghanistan.

Gahnospinel

BLUE SPINEL

This blue, zinc-rich variety of spinel is called gahnospinel, after the Swedish chemist J. G. Gahn.

Black Prince's Ruby

TOPAZ

THE NAME "TOPAZ" is thought to come from the Sanskrit *tapas*, meaning "fire." The stone occurs naturally in a range of different colors and is also heat-treated to produce the more popular hues. Pink topaz, for example, is usually an irradiated form of the more common yellow.

VICTORIAN PENDANT
Pink topaz, peridot, and diamonds sparkle from this Victorian pendant, dating from about 1880.

OCTAGONAL STEP CUT
Although blue topaz does occur naturally, it can also be created by heat-treating a colorless variety.

STEP CUT

Foil-backed gems

NECKLACE
The gemstones in this antique necklace are foil-backed to enhance their color.

The Brazilian Princess weighs over 21,000 carats, or 8.8 lb (4 kg)

PRICELESS
The Brazilian Princess was once the largest gem ever faceted. It is now on display at the Smithsonian Institution, Washington, D.C.

Brilliant   Cushion   Step   Mixed   Pendeloque

HARDNESS 8

PENDELOQUE CUT
It is possible to see tear-shaped inclusions within this cut crystal. They are characteristic of topaz and usually contain bubbles of gas or liquid.

Pink topaz

Diamonds

BROOCH
A large mixed-cut topaz forms the heart of this early-19th-century brooch, framed by 18 cushion-cut diamonds. The outer edge has four more topazes set within diamond foliage.

Brazilian crystal

OVAL MIXED CUT
Color is more important than size in determining the value of topaz. Today, pink, blue, and honey-colored stones are the most sought after.

CRYSTAL
Topaz crystals can be up to 3 ft (1 m) long and weigh several hundred pounds! This pale blue example was mined in Brazil, which is better known for red and honey-toned varieties.

Honey-colored gem

MYTH AND MAGIC
• In 1255, St. Hildegard offered a simple remedy for failing eyesight: steep a topaz in wine for three days and then lightly rub it over the eyes.

• Worn around the neck, topaz was thought to cure madness.

TOPAZ NECKLACE

EMERALD

THE BEAUTIFUL GREEN SHADES of the emerald derive from the presence of chromium and vanadium. Only the finest quality gemstones are transparent and flawless; most have tiny fractures or mineral inclusions known as a "jardin," from the French for garden. It is common practice to oil emeralds to disguise these flaws and enhance the color.

ART DECO RING
A square cut emphasizes the richness of the color by leading the eye into the stone rather than deflecting attention away from it.

Excellent emerald-green color

Emerald band emphasizes structure of insect

SYNTHETIC PENDELOQUE
In the 1930s, American scientist Carroll Chatham greatly improved the process for producing synthetic emeralds. He brewed emerald seed crystals at extreme temperatures for up to a year.

Insects were popular motifs in Victorian jewelry

GRASSHOPPER BROOCH
Lush green emeralds are symbolic of the freshness of nature, and the choice of a grasshopper for this emerald-studded brooch adds to that symbolism.

Pendeloque

Step

Step

Cabochon

ANTIQUE CABOCHON EARRINGS

These Art Deco earrings boast large hanging emeralds. Inclusions – marks either on or within the surface of the stone – are clearly visible, and the carving draws the eye around the surface of the gem rather than into it.

Polished oval cabochons are framed in black enamel

This gem is larger and lighter in color than the other one

Inclusions provide keys to the gem's origins

OCTAGONAL CABOCHON

Emeralds almost always have fissures or inclusions. These may be embedded crystals of other materials, growth lines, or any of a whole range of microscopic occurrences. They tell the story of the gem's origin millions of years ago.

POLISHED PEBBLE

Not all emeralds have to be pried out of rocks. Some find their way into river gravels, where the action of the water tumbles and smooths them so that they resemble shiny pebbles.

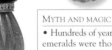

MYTH AND MAGIC

• Hundreds of years ago, emeralds were thought to possess healing powers, particularly for restoring eyesight.

• During the Renaissance, emeralds were exchanged among the aristocracy as symbols – and tests – of friendship; the stone would stay intact only if the friendship lasted.

AQUAMARINE

THE SEAWATER COLOR of aquamarine has given this gemstone its name. In the 19th century, sea-green varieties were the most popular, but blues are more valued today. There are deposits on most continents, although the best quality aquamarines come from Brazil.

PRECIOUS RING
The stone in this early-20th-century ring is step cut to reveal its flawless internal structure. It weighs nearly 21 carats and is worth many thousands of dollars.

BRILLIANT CUT
Depending on the angle at which an aquamarine is viewed, it may appear blue, green, or colorless. This so-called pleochroic effect is enhanced by many small facets.

MYTH AND MAGIC
• In medieval times, this stone was thought to reawaken the love of married couples. It was also believed to render soldiers invincible.

• Aquamarine is known as the sailor's gem, ensuring safe passage across stormy seas.

CABOCHON
The combination of a cabochon cut and growth lines within the crystal structure creates this cat's-eye effect. Six-rayed stars are also sometimes visible.

Fibrous habit contributes to cat's-eye effect

Brilliant

Step   Cabochon

HARDNESS 7–8

OCTAGONAL STEP CUT
Heat-treatment may
enhance or alter the color of a
gemstone and is considered
perfectly acceptable. With
aquamarine, it tends to change
the hue from green to blue.
This untreated stone has a
distinctive greenish tinge.

*Untreated
stone has
greenish hue*

*The layers of
facets are
clearly visible*

UNTREATED, SKY-BLUE STONE
Large crystals of aquamarine are
relatively common. In 1910, one was found
in Brazil weighing 243 lb (110.5 kg), twice
the weight of an average woman!

*Diamonds
set off the
pale blue
aquamarines*

*Brilliant-
cut outer
stones*

CARTIER BROOCH
Designed by the renowned
French jeweler Cartier, this Art
Deco aquamarine and diamond
brooch dates from about 1930. The
two central stones are step cut.

*Unusual,
pendeloque-cut
drop earrings*

ZIRCON

IN THEIR PUREST FORM, zircons are colorless, but more commonly they are golden brown. The name "zircon" is thought to come from the Persian *zargun*, meaning "golden." Although they occur in a range of colors, many zircons are heat-treated to produce the popular blue or colorless varieties.

Brilliant cut enhances color

Brown zircon can turn blue when heated

GOLDEN BROWN
These earrings display the distinctive golden tones of zircons. The brilliant cut adds to their natural fire.

ZIRCON PEBBLES
Gem-quality crystals are usually found as brown pebbles in alluvial deposits in places such as Sri Lanka and Myanmar (Burma). Those on the right have been heat-treated.

HEAT-TREATED ZIRCON

BAGUETTE CUT
This colorless stone started its life as a reddish brown zircon crystal.

BLUE ZIRCON RING
This step-cut zircon is set in a four-claw mount with white gold. It was made in the late 1930s.

Brilliant   Cushion   Baguette   Mixed

HARDNESS 7.5

COLORLESS ZIRCON RING
Clear zircons are frequently sold, intentionally or mistakenly, as diamonds. Zircons display a fire similar to that of diamonds, but are brittle and susceptible to damage, particularly around the edges of the stone.

Zircons cut as rose diamonds

GREEN ZIRCON NECKLACE
In this early-20th-century necklace, 36 step-cut stones are set in silver-gilt mounts to protect them and heighten their color and shine.

Step-cut zircons

Silver-gilt mounts

Indian-style silver setting

BROOCH
The zircons in this floral brooch are naturally colorless. The danger of using heat-treated stones is that under certain conditions they can revert to their original hue.

CUSHION BRILLIANT CUT
In Roman times, golden stones were the most popular and prized. The impurities in zircons can also produce green, blue, red, and yellow varieties.

MYTH AND MAGIC

• Zircons that lost their luster were once thought to be a sign of danger.

• All zircons were deemed magical. In the 14th century, they were popularly worn to safeguard against the Black Death.

TOURMALINE

USUALLY OCCURRING as long, three-sided prisms, tourmalines come in a wide array of colors and an equally large range of varieties. For example, rubellite is red-toned, indicolite is dark blue, and achroite is colorless. Important tourmaline deposits are found in Brazil, California, and the Russian Federation.

Ornate carvings

CHINESE BOTTLE
A pheasant, symbol of prosperity and good fortune, is carved into the tourmaline. This ornate bottle was designed to hold snuff.

ACHROITE
These rare tourmalines are named after the Greek word *achroos*, meaning "without color."

STEP-CUT RUBELLITE
In 1777, King Gustavus III of Sweden presented a deep red tourmaline to the Russian empress Catherine the Great, believing it to be a priceless ruby.

Cushion   Cameo   Brilliant   Step

HARDNESS 7–7.5

MUSEUM PIECES

These earrings are copies of an early-19th-century design. The originals would probably have been made with emeralds. Green tourmaline is fairly common and is known as verdelite.

Verdelite tourmaline

Brilliant cut

WATERMELON TOURMALINE

Many tourmaline crystals are multicolored. The watermelon variety is rarely used in jewelry.

DRAVITE

Dark brown tourmalines are rich in magnesium. They can be lightened by heat-treatment.

Cushion mixed-cut dravite

SCHORL

Black tourmalines are very common. They used to be popular for mourning jewelry during Victorian times.

Schorl is rich in iron

SCHORL CRYSTAL

Domed tourmaline

PURPLE PENDANT

Held by a diamond-studded "ribbon," this domed purple tourmaline is exceptionally large, measuring 37 mm across.

MYTH AND MAGIC

• In the 18th century, a Dutch scientist claimed that a tourmaline wrapped in silk and placed against the cheek of a feverish child would induce sleep.

GARNET

A NUMBER OF GEMSTONES sharing a similar cubic crystal structure and chemical composition make up the garnet family. The color of these varies greatly, although the name "garnet" comes from the Latin for pomegranate, which has bright red, garnetlike seeds.

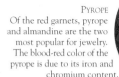

Circular and pear-shaped stones

VICTORIAN EARRINGS

The gold design on these drop earrings represents the arms and neck of an amphora (a Greek or Roman storage vessel).

Unusual rounded pendeloques

MYTH AND MAGIC

• In medieval times, garnets were thought to cure depression, protect against bad dreams, and relieve diseases of the liver and hemorrhages.

• According to legend, Noah used a finely cut, glowing garnet to illuminate the ark.

PYROPE

Of the red garnets, pyrope and almandine are the two most popular for jewelry. The blood-red color of the pyrope is due to its iron and chromium content.

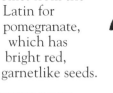

Brilliant Step Cabochon Mixed

HARDNESS 6.5–7.5

SPESSARTINE
It is rare to find gem-quality spessartine, and this example has characteristic inclusions.

Liquid inclusions

Brilliant cut enhances violet color

ALMANDINE
Almandine tends to have a violet tint. As well as its use in jewelry, almandine was once incorporated into church and temple stained-glass windows.

Green demantoid garnets

LIZARD BROOCH
In Europe, the lizard is often regarded as a love charm and is a symbol of renewal. Here demantoids, the most valuable of the garnet family, form the body.

GARNET NECKLACE
Dating from about 1820, this necklace has a flower motif with rosette clusters and decorative leaves set in gold.

QUARTZ

ROCK CRYSTAL, ROSE QUARTZ, and citrine all belong to the quartz family. Rock crystal is the purest of these; its name derives from *krustallos*, the Greek word for ice, as the stone was originally thought to be a type of ice created by the gods. Rose quartz is rose-tinted, caused by traces of titanium; citrine is a golden version of quartz and is colored by its iron content.

Faceted rock crystal

CRYSTAL BEADS
Rock crystal beads come in a variety of shapes and finishes. They may be carved, frosted, or, as here, faceted and highly polished.

CHINESE BOTTLE
This crystal snuff bottle dates from about 1800. The design incorporates a dragon carved in relief on each side. In China, dragons represent the highest spiritual power.

FLOWER BROOCH
The carving in this piece is typical of work produced in Germany in the 1920s and 1930s. Rock crystal has been carved into a flower head and then frosted, with a diamond in the center.

Gold leaf

CRYSTAL BROOCH

CRYSTAL BOTTLE

Bead

Cameo

Brilliant

MYTH AND MAGIC

• Throughout the world, crystal balls have been used to see into the future.

• Citrine is reputed to be an unlucky stone.

• Crystal healing is an ancient art. It works on the principle that certain crystals give off powerful, much-needed energy for the body.

Crystals are typically cloudy

ROSE CRYSTALS

Pink or peach-colored quartz is known as rose quartz. It tends to be cloudy, and certain varieties produce a star effect when cut as a cabochon. In ancient Rome, the stone was popular for making seals.

ROSE-TINTED EARRINGS

Pale pink flower heads are framed by silver leaves in these contemporary British earrings. Rose quartz tends to be brittle, so larger carvings may show cracks. It is also prone to fading over time.

Carved crystal

ROSE QUARTZ

Faceted beads

GOLDEN BEADS

Citrine's name derives from its color – *citron* being the French for lemon. Gem-quality citrine is extremely rare. Large pieces may be carved as pendants; smaller ones, made into beads.

CITRINE NECKLACE

CITRINE DROPS

The best citrine is mined in Brazil, although many of the stones sold as citrines today are in fact heat-treated amethysts. At 878° F (470° C), amethysts produce pale yellow stones. At higher temperatures, the yellow becomes darker.

AMETHYST

OCCURRING IN shades of purple, lilac, and mauve, this is the most valuable of the quartz group. Some amethyst is heat-treated to produce the yellow variety of quartz known as citrine. Amethyst is traditionally thought to have strong talismanic properties; amethyst crystals are still used in forms of natural healing.

GRAPES
In myth, Bacchus, Roman god of wine, caused a maiden named Amethyst to be turned into rock crystal. In horror at what he had done, he threw down his goblet of wine, coloring the crystal a beautiful violet.

AMETHYST GRAPES BROOCH

AMETHYST CRYSTAL AND ROCK CRYSTAL
Here amethyst crystals grow from a bed of rock crystal. Structurally, amethyst is simply a colored – containing impurities – form of rock crystal. The color is often darker at the end of the crystal.

Characteristic pyramid formation

CABOCHON CUFF LINK
These cabochons are notable for their hexagonal cut; most cabochons are either round or oval.

Baguette	Bead	Mixed

7 6

DROP EARRINGS
These elegant earrings consist of pendeloque-cut amethysts. Usually, deep-colored stones are faceted to accentuate their color, while paler or poorer quality ones are cut into cabochons.

Pale-colored amethyst

VICTORIAN NECKLACE
The stones of this necklace appear darker than their natural color because they are backed and surrounded by gold. In the early 19th century, it was not uncommon to place foil behind gemstones in order to enhance their color.

Enclosed gold setting

MIXED-CUT RING
Amethysts owe their color to the presence of iron, and deep tones tend to be the most favored. Rich sources of good-quality crystals come from Russia's Ural Mountains, Brazil, and Uruguay.

Delicate diamond frame

FLORAL SPRAY
Nine dark purple crystals have been carved into delicate petals, each flower being made of a single stone inlaid with a central diamond. The brooch is mounted in platinum and 18-carat gold and is signed by its American designer, William Ruser.

Five petals carved from a single stone

MYTH AND MAGIC
• Amethysts were thought to induce a sober mind; the name is derived from the Greek word *amethystos*, which means "against drunkenness."

• In traditional Chinese medicine, ground amethyst is prescribed for stomach pains and bad dreams.

CHALCEDONY

THE GROUP OF QUARTZES that includes agate, chrysoprase, carnelian, jasper, and bloodstone makes up the family of gemstones known as "chalcedony." They are linked by their microcrystalline structure and waxy or dull appearance. Apple-green chrysoprase is the most valuable of these and has been mined since the 14th century.

Athena, Greek goddess of wisdom and war

SARDONYX CAMEO RING
Layer stones such as sardonyx make ideal gems for cameos. Here the white has been carved away to reveal a helmeted Athena.

Opaque stone

JASPER
This stone is usually striped, spotted, or multi-colored – it is rarely all one color. Boulders of jasper can weigh up to several hundred pounds.

JASPER SLAB

MYTH AND MAGIC

• In the Middle Ages, bloodstone was thought to hold drops of Christ's blood and to be all-powerful.

• In Renaissance times, sardonyx was worn by wives to bring about marital happiness.

Characteristic red spots and veins

BLOODSTONE
Polished slabs of bloodstone are often used decoratively as inlay or as cameos. The red spots in this stone are due to traces of iron oxides.

Cabochon

Bead

Cameo   Polished

HARDNESS 7

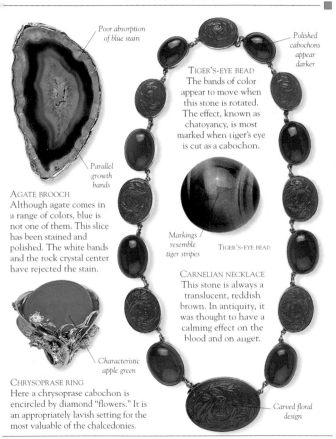

Poor absorption of blue stain

Parallel growth bands

AGATE BROOCH
Although agate comes in a range of colors, blue is not one of them. This slice has been stained and polished. The white bands and the rock crystal center have rejected the stain.

Polished cabochons appear darker

TIGER'S-EYE BEAD
The bands of color appear to move when this stone is rotated. The effect, known as chatoyancy, is most marked when tiger's eye is cut as a cabochon.

Markings resemble tiger stripes

TIGER'S-EYE BEAD

CARNELIAN NECKLACE
This stone is always a translucent, reddish brown. In antiquity, it was thought to have a calming effect on the blood and on anger.

Characteristic apple green

CHRYSOPRASE RING
Here a chrysoprase cabochon is encircled by diamond "flowers." It is an appropriately lavish setting for the most valuable of the chalcedonies.

Carved floral design

JADE

TWO DISTINCT MINERALS, jadeite and nephrite, are recognized as jade. Nephrite is the more common and has been carved for thousands of years. Jadeite is slightly harder, often appears dimpled when polished, and comes in virtually every color.

CARVED JADEITE
This Chinese pomander once contained aromatic substances. It is suspended from a tourmaline bead and string of seed pearls.

JADEITE
Black inclusions can be seen throughout this polished jadeite pebble. It is translucent with a greasy luster.

Jadeite beads

IMPERIAL JADE
This unusually long string of beads is of the finest quality jadeite, known as imperial jade, typified by its rich, emerald-green hue.

MYTH AND MAGIC

• In China, children wore small jade amulets to prevent disease.

• Powdered and distilled in dew water, jade was believed to calm the mind.

• Its name comes from the Spanish *piedra de hijada*, loin stone, since jade was thought to cure hip problems.

Rich imperial green shade

Bead   Cameo   Polished

HARDNESS 6.5–7

YELLOW JADE
Carved in the shape of a purse with drawstrings, this Chinese pomander is worked in fine, yellow-toned jadeite. Each side is decorated with an insect hovering over flowering sprigs.

Seven-character inscription

Even white color

WHITE JADE
The base of this intricate box is carved in the shape of two peaches joined together on a leafy branch. Its white color results from the absence of iron.

Box cover depicts descending crane

CHINESE CAMEL
Here the artist used the shape of the stone for inspiration. With minimal carving, he transformed the nephrite into a resting camel.

WHITE NEPHRITE CAMEL

JADEITE BANGLE
Jade is an extremely tough gemstone despite being only 7 on Mohs' scale of hardness. This is due to its structure – a mass of tiny interlocking grains and fibers.

ANTIQUE BEADS
The lilac coloring of this jadeite necklace is due to traces of manganese. Knots prevent the beads from damaging one another.

LILAC BEADS

PERIDOT

THE MOST IMPORTANT deposits of peridot are on the so-called "serpent isle" – the volcanic island of Zebirget in the Red Sea. According to Greek legend, vicious snakes lived on the island, guarding the precious stone and killing anyone who dared to approach it.

Step-cut drop

PERIDOTS AND DIAMONDS
Peridot's rich, oily green color depends on its iron content. The stone is often cut as a pendeloque, as on the left, to create a darker, more favored, hue.

OVAL MIXED CUT
Peridot has strong double refraction, which means that you can often see a doubling of the back facets.

MYTH AND MAGIC

• The early Egyptians claimed that peridot glowed by night but was invisible by day.

• In the Middle Ages, peridot was believed to dispel the darkness and terrors of the night.

• King Edward VII of England used to wear a peridot for good luck.

Intaglio design – carved inward

CARVED SIGNET RING
This ring is probably of Roman origin and would have been commissioned by the man who is featured. He would have used it to seal his letters.

| Step | Cabochon | Table | Cameo | Pendeloque |

STRINGS OF BEADS
Peridot is the name given to gem-quality specimens of the mineral olivine. Olivine derives its name from its characteristic olive-green color, although it can also be bottle green or yellowish green. This peridot necklace displays a variety of shades.

Varying shades of green

4-mm round beads

Diamonds frame central stone

LINKED BRACELET
This 20th-century bracelet is made of seven oval, step-cut stones. Peridot was once known as "evening emerald," but with a hardness of 6.5, is much less durable than its more illustrious cousin.

White gold setting for diamonds; yellow gold for peridot

Foliate design

DROP EARRINGS
Peridots are usually set in gold to complement their color. Here a combination of white and yellow gold has been used, with white gold for the diamonds. The earrings form part of a set with the pendant opposite (top left).

Elongated gold beads form the links

MOONSTONE

REMINISCENT OF the silvery moon, this stone derives its name from its blue-white sheen. Indeed, it was once thought that the gem's luster waxed and waned just like the moon itself, and moonstones have always been used in jewelry by moon-worshipers. In reality, the stone's distinctive sheen comes from its structure: thin albite layers create an attractive blue; thicker layers, a more milky opalescence.

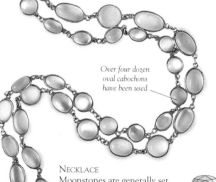

The stones have a bluish sheen

Over four dozen oval cabochons have been used

CUSHION BRILLIANT CUT
The relative flatness of the cushion cut refracts the light in such a way as to enhance the opalescence of the stone.

NECKLACE
Moonstones are generally set in silver, which brings out their characteristic bluish-silvery sheen.

Cushion   Cabochon   Cameo

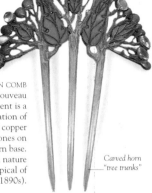

EASTERN EARRINGS
These earrings from
Afghanistan show the
moonstone's range of
hues. The hanging
drops are considerably
lighter than the four
upper ones.

*The single drops
are "moon-
colored"*

HORN COMB
This Art Nouveau
hair ornament is a
combination of
enameled copper
and moonstones on
a carved horn base.
Designs from nature
were typical of
the period (1890s).

*Carved horn
"tree trunks"*

CUFF LINKS
Large cabochons form the sides of
these cuff links, designed by Carl
Fabergé ca. 1910. The moonstones'
pink sheen is due to the setting.

*Gold setting
lends a golden,
pinkish tinge*

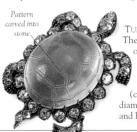

*Pattern
carved into
stone*

TURTLE BROOCH
The distinctive markings
of the turtle's upper
shell are carved into
the moonstone in
this unusual piece
(ca. 1900). The
diamonds set in the legs
and head are cushion cut.

MYTH AND MAGIC
• In India, the
moonstone is believed
to bring good luck and
is considered sacred.
• The Romans thought
that the wearers of
moonstones would
receive wisdom, wealth,
and success in battle.

OPAL

UNLIKE OTHER GEMSTONES, the opal is non-crystalline and is formed from a hardened silica gel. It is known for its rainbow iridescence. The name "opal" is thought to be derived from the Sanskrit *upala*, meaning "precious stone." The opals used in ancient times came from the former Czechoslovakia, but today most are mined in Australia.

Large black opal

EDWARDIAN RING
Here the opal is cut as a cabochon and reveals a milky-blue iridescence. The ring dates from the early 1900s.

SAMURAI PENDANT
Precious opal with a dark background, as in this unusual Art Deco pendant, is known as black opal. Here the "face" is dark, matching the stone below, while that on the other side is lighter.

MYTH AND MAGIC

• In Europe, the opal is regarded as unlucky. Its reputation dates from the 14th century when many thought it had caused the plague known as the Black Death.

• In Asia, the stone is viewed more favorably. It is a symbol of hope.

UNMOUNTED BLACK OPAL
Despite displaying a predominance of light colors, this uncut stone is of precious black opal. It weighs more than 9 carats.

Silica structure disperses color

Cameo

Step

Cabochon

HARDNESS 5.5–6.5

BROOCH
Milky opal cabochons are interspersed with diamonds in this classically elegant bar pin. The opals show flashes of pale pinks, blues, and greens.

Opal cabochons ranged in decreasing size

Fossilized shell

OPALIZED FOSSIL
Opal is found in fossilized shell, wood, and bone. In this shell, the play of color is caused by the diffraction of light off its closely packed silica spheres.

Diamonds frame the large opals

WINGS OF A BUTTERFLY
Victorian designs paid homage to nature. Moths, bumblebees, and dragonflies were especially popular. Here four large opals form the delicate wings of a butterfly.

FIRE OPAL
Named for their deep orange color, most fire opals are translucent or transparent. They are extremely fragile and suffer from changes in temperature, humidity, and even light intensity.

Shimmering bands of color

TURQUOISE

FIRST MINED OVER 6,000 years ago, turquoise has a rich and colorful history. To the Aztecs, it was the "stone of the gods," used extensively in forms or worship; in medieval times, it was deemed a powerful talisman. Today most commercial turquoise comes from China and the southwestern United States.

CHILD'S NECKLACE
Turquoise forms in solid grapelike masses and as nodules, often containing dark veins, as can be seen here. White enameled links join the stones in this unusual Italian piece.

Floral motif engraved in gold

MYTH AND MAGIC

• Turquoise has always been considered lucky, capable of safeguarding and bringing happiness.

• According to a 15th-century legend, the stone loses its color when its owner is unwell or in danger and regains its brilliance when the illness or danger has passed.

PERSIAN BLUE
Inlaid with gold leaf, this good-luck charm is of the finest sky-blue turquoise, which is mined in Iran. Its distinctive color comes from the presence of copper. Traces of iron cause a greenish tint.

Bead   Cabochon   Cameo

HARDNESS 5–6

RABBIT EARRINGS
In China, turquoise beads are often carved into a variety of animal shapes, as in these contemporary rabbit earrings. Here the silver "feathers" lend them a distinctly American Indian flavor.

Vast turquoise stone set in gold

MAMMOTH RING
The color of turquoise is affected by heat, as well as by oils, cosmetics, and perspiration, and is liable to go from blue to a dull green. In order to minimize the risk of damage, it is best to remove turquoise rings before washing hands.

Hundreds of cabochons form the body

SERPENT NECKLACE
The serpent was a favorite motif for necklaces in Victorian times. When coiled around the base of the throat in a complete circle, it symbolized eternal love.

LIZARD
Turquoise cabochons surround a spine of diamonds in this 19th-century brooch. The eyes are set with brilliant-cut rubies to make them stand out.

Lizard with 45 small turquoises

LAPIS LAZULI

PRIZED FOR ITS INTENSE BLUE color, lapis lazuli has been used in jewelry, carvings, and amulets for thousands of years. Its name derives from medieval Latin and means "blue stone." The Egyptians regarded lapis as a heavenly stone and often used it on the statues of their gods and in burial masks as protection for the next life.

LUCKY HAND
This pendant is doubly powerful – the lapis offers protection against evil, and the clenched fist is a good-luck charm.

ROCK
Lapis is made up of several minerals, but its main ingredient is lazurite. The best quality lapis has a high proportion of lazurite.

White calcite

Dragon-head hook

CARVED LAPIS
This dragon garment hook is carved in high relief. The many tiny crystals in lapis make it an ideal material for carving.

IMITATION LAPIS
The French manufacturer Pierre Gilson created an artificial lapis using lazurite. The imitation stone has a composition similar to that of natural lapis, but is slightly softer.

Cabochon   Cameo   Polished

HARDNESS 5–5.5

TIFFANY NECKLACE
The American jeweler Tiffany designed this fine lapis and jade necklace. The beads are carved, and every alternate one is cupped in gold filigree. The lapis is of a rich, dark blue variety.

Sulfur gives rich blue color

Single bead of blue jade

Thickly cut slices of lapis

CONTEMPORARY EARRINGS
Lapis is hard enough to take a good polish. These stones come from the United States, which is known for its dark, high-quality lapis. Afghanistan is another important source.

Intricately carved surface

CARTIER BANGLE
Dating from the 1950s, this carved bangle is the work of the Parisian design house Cartier. The piece is in the form of a chimera – a mythical fire-breathing monster.

Carved from a single piece of lapis

MYTH AND MAGIC
• Both the ancient Egyptians and Babylonians believed that lapis lazuli could cure melancholy.

• Today, lapis is used in Chinese medicine to treat phlegm, congestion, and spasms.

AZURITE AND MALACHITE

THESE TWO STONES have a similar chemistry and history. Both are copper-based, both have been crushed and used as pigments, and both have been worked for thousands of years. The ancient Egyptians wore malachite as jewelry and used azurite for carving ornaments.

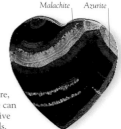

Malachite *Azurite*

Azurite "donut"

AZURITE PENDANT
Azurite derives its name from its azure-blue color. It is typically used for ornamental objects and simple jewelry, such as this circular pendant.

POLISHED AZURITE
Azurite often intergrows with malachite, creating fabulous color effects. Here, bands of green malachite can be seen with the distinctive bright blue azurite crystals.

Characteristic azure blue

MYTH AND MAGIC
• During the Middle Ages, malachite was used as a cure for vomiting.

• Worn by children, malachite was thought to protect them and to keep evil spirits at bay.

• The ancient Egyptians used malachite amulets to ward off evil.

AZURITE

Cameo   Cabochon

ROCK OF AZURITE
Azurite occurs as short crystals or in spherical lumps, as here. Copper gives the stone its distinctive color.

HARDNESS 3.5–4

NECKLACE AND EARRINGS
Malachite is almost always set in silver, as the two colors work well together. Here, polished cabochons are set within hexagonal silver frames. The stones are similar, but irregular.

Silver setting

CLIP EARRINGS

WILD ANIMAL BROOCH
This piece, with its beautifully modeled elephant and giraffe, takes jewelry into the realm of wearable art. The base, a slab of polished malachite, forms a perfect ground for the animals.

Alternating light and dark greens

MALACHITE BROOCH

Circular bands of color

MALACHITE SLAB
The round and kidney-shaped formations are characteristic of this stone. Large pieces of a single color are rare.

POLISHED SLAB

MALACHITE NECKLACE

Polished "pebbles"

ORGANIC GEMSTONES

PEARL 96
CORAL 98
JET 100
IVORY 102
AMBER 104
SHELL 106

PEARL

ONCE VIEWED BY ARABS as tears of the gods, pearls are created by certain shellfish, mainly oysters and mussels. They form when an irritant such as a grain of sand enters the shell. The mollusk then secretes layer upon layer of calcium carbonate, known as nacre, around the foreign body. It is this innate defense mechanism that creates the bead of pearl.

NATURAL PEARL IN OYSTER SHELL
The term "natural pearl" refers to a pearl that has formed as an accident of nature and not by human intervention. Such pearls are rare and valuable.

The pearl is still attached to the shell lining

SEED-PEARL BRACELET
Pearls vary in size from a millimeter in diameter to as large as a pigeon's egg! Their weight is given in grains, 1 grain = 0.002 oz (0.05 g). Seed pearls weigh less than 0.25 grain.

Perfect size, form, and color

CULTURED PEARLS
It is virtually impossible to find natural pearls that match. This string is of cultured pearls, produced artificially by inserting beads of clam shell into oysters.

Strings of cultured seed pearls

Bead

So-called black pearls are gun-metal colored

Triton, son of Poseidon, Greek god of the seas

Small baroque pearl

Natural pearls take up to seven years to form

GRAPE EARRINGS

The multicolored pearls in these early-20th-century earrings are probably produced by Tahitian Black Lip oysters. These oysters secrete a dark pigment directly into the pearly strata.

CANNING JEWEL

Irregularly shaped pearls are known as baroque pearls. The 16th-century Triton has four, with the largest one forming the body. It is fitting that a sea god is made up of pearls – the "fruits" of the sea.

Cultured pearls take up to four years to form

Classic cream-white color

MYTH AND MAGIC

• According to the Roman writer Pliny, Cleopatra dissolved a priceless pearl earring in her wine and drank it as a testament of love for Antony.

• Pearls have long been used medicinally. They were thought to cure everything from fevers to stomach ulcers.

CORAL

MOST CORAL – red, pink, white, and blue varieties – consists of a substance similar to that of pearls, calcium carbonate, but that is where the similarity ends. Coral is formed by the build up of skeletal remains of colonies of tiny marine animals known as coral polyps. It grows in branchlike formations.

Hand of good luck

RED CORAL
This sprig of red coral comes from the warm waters of the Mediterranean. It has a distinctive "wood-grain" pattern on the surface of its branches.

CHILD'S BRACELET
Coral was thought to protect the wearer against evil; children in particular were given coral jewelry to ensure their safety and keep them healthy.

Branch-like structure

CORAL FRAGMENT NECKLACE
Large pieces of coral are relatively rare and so are saved for decorative objects or cameos. Branches too small for beads may be fashioned into "sprig" strings.

POLISHED CABOCHON
Coral has been used in jewelry for thousands of years. The deeper the color, the more prized the coral.

Bead   Cabochon   Cameo

HARDNESS 3

Highly polished cabochon

BLACK CORAL
Black and golden corals differ structurally from other varieties. They are composed of an organic, hornlike substance called conchiolin.

AFRICAN NECKLACE
Unworked coral has a dull, horny appearance. For coral to become "gem" quality, its outer crust has to be removed. The coral is then cut, usually with a saw or knife, shaped as desired, and polished.

Hundreds of rough corals

WHITE CORAL BROOCH
A large oval cabochon is framed by diamonds and ten white coral beads in this gold-mounted brooch. In the early 1900s, it was fashionable to marry the humble coral with the world's rarest and most precious gemstone.

PALE PINK
Graduated cabochons of the palest pink are interspersed with diamonds in this ring, which dates from about 1900. It was probably given as a 35th-wedding-anniversary present.

Monkey on a blossom tree

MONKEY CARVING
The relative softness of coral means that it is quite easy to carve. This piece is of Eastern origin; much pink coral is taken from the waters around Japan.

MYTH AND MAGIC
• In the 16th century, people thought that a sprig of red or white coral could calm a raging tempest;
• Coral allegedly cured madness and protected against enchantments.

JET

A PRODUCT OF FOSSILIZED WOOD, jet is similar to coal, only harder and more durable. Jet forms when the remains of wood are immersed in stagnant water for hundreds of years and then buried and compacted under intense pressure. In the 19th century, jet became popular for mourning jewelry, because of its color. Glass, onyx, and a type of rubber known as vulcanite are used as imitation jet.

Whitby jet

JET BRACELET
Faceted, flat, oval plates of jet are strung together in this polished 19th-century bangle.

SYMBOLIC BROOCH
The dove symbolizes peace and salvation. Here it is coupled with a heart, an emblem of love, in this finely carved remembrance brooch.

Carved jet

DOVE OF PEACE

BLACK ROSE
Jet from Whitby, Yorkshire, is considered the best quality, because it takes such a good polish. This piece dates from the late 19th century and features a rose. It would have been worn by a woman in mourning.

Polished

Bead

Cameo

HARDNESS 2.5

BEADED CLOTH
This delicate trim from a Victorian overskirt has beads of faceted jet sewn into the fabric, as was the fashion of the day. The beads create a gem-studded form of black lace, the scallop design edged by rows of black sequins.

ACORNS
Queen Victoria of England popularized jet by wearing it after the death of her husband, Prince Albert. Death was viewed as a passage into another life, and this acorn (which forms part of a necklace) reflects that sense of hope and renewal.

Trim of drilled jet beads

HAIR COMB
At its height of fashion, Whitby jet was exported all over Europe. Combs were popular in Spain, where they were used to hold up a lady's black mantilla – a lace veil worn in church.

Jet hair comb

MYTH AND MAGIC

• According to the Roman writer Pliny, jet mixed with the marrow of a stag could heal a serpent's bite.

• Powdered and mixed with beeswax, jet was used to shrink tumors, and mixed with wine, to alleviate toothache.

• In China, jet is a symbol of winter.

IVORY

THE TERM "IVORY" is generally associated with elephant tusks, although it also includes the teeth or tusks of such mammals as the hippopotamus, boar, sea lion, and sperm whale. People have collected ivory for thousands of years, prizing it for its rich creamy color and fine texture. It has always been a popular material for jewelry, ornaments, and amulets.

String of graduated beads

AFRICAN NECKLACE
Polished elephant ivory, such as the beads on this necklace, is characterized by a distinct cross-hatch pattern in the grain called engine turning.

Stylized crocodile

BROOCH
This 20th-century brooch was carved on the shores of Lake Malawi, an area known for crocodiles. As in many other parts of the world, Malawi has strict restrictions on the sale of ivory.

PATCHWORK BOX
Ivory is quite a soft material to work with and, because of its porous nature, can be dyed easily. Here slices of natural and stained ivory create a decorative surface for this small box.

INLAID BOX

| Bead | Cameo | Polished |

HARDNESS 2.5

POLISHED SECTION OF ELEPHANT TOOTH
This ivory slice is a horizontal cross-section of an Indian elephant's molar tooth. The white bands are enamel and the yellowish bands are dentine. The dark lines are cracks that occurred when the tooth dried out after the elephant died.

Crack

MOLAR TOOTH

Ivory face with ruby eyes

DEVIL HAT PIN
Dating from around 1840, this ivory hat pin is carved in the form of Lucifer's face, complete with gold horns and piercing ruby eyes. Like the more common carved skull, it is a memento mori – a playful reminder of human mortality.

Uniformly carved beads

CARVED BEADS
These carved beads have a distinctly organic feel, resembling a rare tropical fruit. The necklace is of African origin, although India, Myanmar (Burma), and Indonesia are also significant sources of elephant ivory.

AMBER

FORMED FROM THE fossilized resin of trees that lived millions of years ago, amber has been used for jewelry and religious objects since prehistoric times. It was believed to have talismanic properties, and many ancient peoples buried amber objects and amulets with their dead to protect them in the afterlife. It is usually a golden orange color.

Insect and spider trapped in resin

PENDANT
Plants and insects may become trapped in the sticky resin before it sets. In this extraordinary pendant from London's Natural History Museum, a spider and a cricket are visible.

Rough pebble found washed up on beach

BALTIC AMBER
Most commercial amber comes from the Baltic coasts of Poland and the former USSR, although other notable deposits are in Sicily, Myanmar (Burma), and the Dominican Republic. Amber tends to be found in soft sediments or in the sea. It is occasionally washed ashore after heavy storms.

GOLDEN BEADS
These honey-toned, antique beads are of an opaque variety and have aged well. Amber has a tendency to dry out and crack if left in the sun or worn in the heat of the day.

Bead

Cabochon

Cameo

Polished

DANISH AMBER
This fossilized pebble is a mixture of clear and cloudy amber and was found along the Danish coast. Amber is not as dense as synthetic and plastic resins and will float in saltwater.

Cloudy, opaque areas

DARK RED BEADS
The rich red tones of this necklace suggest that the amber originated in China; Baltic examples tend to be pale yellow or golden. More than 50 drilled, faceted, and polished beads have been used.

Chinese amber

ELECTRIC CHARGE
This translucent bead has a resinous luster and hints of cracks. Amber is known for producing an electrical charge when rubbed. It is from the Greek name for amber, *elektron*, that the word "electricity" is derived.

GOLDEN GRAPES
Amber's relative softness makes it easy to carve, as can be seen in the glistening grapes that dangle from the overhanging leaf. This brooch is of Baltic origin.

DROP EARRINGS
These amber and gold earrings are of Italian design. The air bubbles and inclusions give amber its characteristic mottled appearance and are not seen as flaws. However, this opaqueness can be removed by boiling the fossil resin in oil.

MYTH AND MAGIC
• Sacred to the Greek sun god Apollo, amber was once thought to be congealed sunlight.

• Amber was also viewed as tears – for the Vikings, Freya's tears for Svipdag; and for the ancient Greeks, tears over the death of Phaeton.

SHELL

THESE OFFERINGS from the sea have been used as items of adornment for thousands of years. Conch shells, with their pink and white layers, have been fashioned into cameos since Roman times, and the use of mother-of-pearl, the iridescent lining of many shells, goes back still further. Tortoiseshell, the hard shell of the hawksbill turtle, has been made into countless boxes, bangles, and hair ornaments over the years.

CAMEO
This cameo dates from ca. 1900. It was common then for cameos to reflect classical scenes, paying homage to ancient empires.

TIGER COWRIE CAMEO
To create a cameo, layers of shell are carved away to reveal the different colors. It takes great skill to create a realistic image.

Mottled colors

HAIR COMB
At one time, tortoiseshell was the most popular material for hair ornaments, such as this comb. Today, because of overhunting, most combs are made of plastic.

TIGER COWRIE SHELL

Cabochon   Cameo   Polished

HARDNESS 2.5

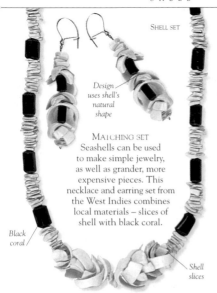

SHELL SET

Design uses shell's natural shape

MATCHING SET
Seashells can be used to make simple jewelry, as well as grander, more expensive pieces. This necklace and earring set from the West Indies combines local materials – slices of shell with black coral.

Black coral

Shell slices

TREASURE BOX
Here, a silver lid and clasp have transformed this shell into a box. The shell is of the "turban" family and comes from the Indian Ocean; the green tones are not natural but the result of a dye.

Dyed shell

Silver lid

PAUA-SHELL BROOCH
Paua is a blue shell from the shores of New Zealand. It is part of the abalone family, but characteristically has far richer tones of blues, greens, and purples. Here a cabochon from the mother-of-pearl lining has been framed in copper and silver.

MYTH AND MAGIC
• In China, mother-of-pearl has been prescribed for over 1,000 years. It is used for heart palpitations, dizziness, and high blood pressure.

• Venus, goddess of love, is believed to have emerged from the sea in a giant scallop shell.

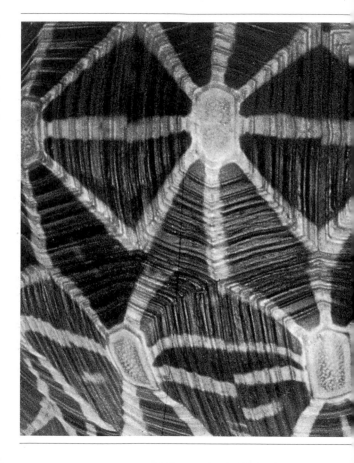

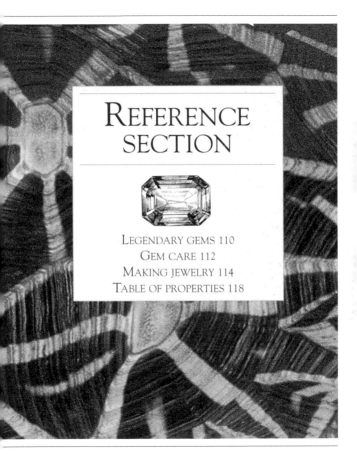

REFERENCE SECTION

LEGENDARY GEMS 110
GEM CARE 112
MAKING JEWELRY 114
TABLE OF PROPERTIES 118

LEGENDARY GEMS

IT IS NO WONDER that there are so many stories surrounding gemstones. They represent money and glamour, desired by all, but owned by few. Precious stones have been the cause of countless thefts, strange events, and even murders, some of which are recounted here.

THE BOLDNESS OF CAPTAIN BLOOD
During the reign of Charles II of England (1660–85), Blood, a former army officer, attempted to steal the crown jewels from the Tower of London. Disguised as a parson, he befriended the Master of the Jewel-House. Then one day he and his friends bludgeoned the 80-year-old warder with a mallet and seized the royal regalia. However, the burglary was interrupted by the arrival of the warder's son, who raised the alarm. The thieves headed for the wharf with their booty, dropping the scepter in their haste, but were overtaken, and the crown, globe, and scepter were returned to their rightful place.

TOWER OF LONDON

MISTAKEN IDENTITY
In 1740 a gigantic diamond was found in Brazil, valued at millions of dollars. The stone became the prized property of the Braganza's, the Portuguese royal family, and then disappeared from view. It is believed to have been set in the Portuguese crown jewels. If this is the case, then the famous Braganza Diamond is in fact only a humble, albeit beautiful, aquamarine.

MODEL OF THE BRAGANZA

THE CAT'S-EYE CATASTROPHE
The French queen Marie Antoinette gave a massive cat's-eye ring to a devoted admirer of hers – the Swedish count Axel de Fersen. After her death during the French Revolution, Count Fersen never removed the ring from his left hand, and he was wearing it when

he was stoned to death on the steps of Stockholm Cathedral some years later. One of his attackers allegedly hacked his finger off with an ax, and threw the ring, finger and all, into the sea. But the ring returned to haunt the man, who imagined he was being threatened by a disembodied hand.

MARIE ANTOINETTE

A JINXED JEWEL

King Alfonso XII of Spain jilted his fiancée, the countess of Castiglione, in favor of a princess of royal blood. The Countess sent her betrayer a wedding present of a superb opal, knowing it to be a stone of ill-omen. Within months, Alfonso's new bride was dead. The king then gave the ring to his grandmother, and she, too, died. His sister soon followed, and finally King Alfonso himself fell victim to the opal's curse.

MYSTERY THEFT

On October 14, 1946, the jewel box of the duchess of Windsor was stolen from her stately

DUKE AND DUCHESS OF WINDSOR

home in Ednam, England. Strangely, the duchess's dog did not bark, the jewels were under her maid's bed rather than safely under lock and key, and none of the stated contents of the case were ever recovered. Nevertheless, the insurers paid the full amount of the claim – about $100,000 – and the delighted duchess was able to buy the first of her Cartier panther jewels, a brooch of a big cat on a magnificent 90-carat emerald cushion.

CARTIER PANTHER

SMASH AND GRAB

In August 1958, the illustrious New York jeweler Tiffany & Co. was the victim of a daring robbery. Early one Sunday morning, two men leaped out of a car and smashed the store windows. In just minutes, they grabbed thousands of dollars' worth of diamonds. The jewels were never recovered.

LIPPERT'S LUGGAGE

In September 1989, Felice Lippert, co-founder of Weight Watchers International, mysteriously lost her handbag containing $500,000 worth of uninsured jewelry. At Miami's Palm Beach airport, she placed her bag on the X-ray machine's conveyor belt, and the bag disappeared, never to be seen again!

GEM CARE

GEMSTONES HAVE LASTED for millions of years underground. However, once mined and made into jewelry, they are exposed to conditions and chemicals that can affect their life spans. Precious stones may fracture, break, lose their shine, or even change color if they are not cared for properly.

STORAGE OF GEMSTONES

Store each piece separately, as harder gemstones, such as diamonds and rubies, will scratch softer ones. Particular care should be taken with the organics, as they are all extremely soft and liable to damage. Jewelry should be kept in individual boxes, in compartments in a jewelry box, or wrapped in cloth or tissue paper.

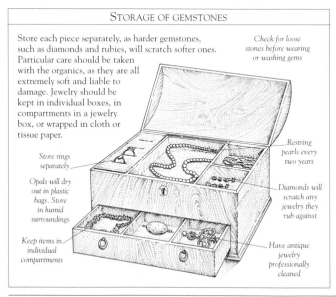

Check for loose stones before wearing or washing gems

Store rings separately

Opals will dry out in plastic bags. Store in humid surroundings

Keep items in individual compartments

Restring pearls every two years

Diamonds will scratch any jewelry they rub against

Have antique jewelry professionally cleaned

CARE AND CLEANING OF GEMSTONES

Remove jewelry before doing any gardening or housework. Clean gems regularly using warm water and bar soap, or a dilute vinegar solution, unless specific instructions are given below. Dishwashing liquid is too harsh to use on organic gems. It should also be avoided with emeralds and rubies, since it will strip them of any oil that may have been applied. Never wear organic gems in swimming pools.

SOAP

TOOTHBRUSH

SOFT CLOTH

DISHWASHING LIQUID

BOWL

ORGANIC GEMSTONES	
Pearl	Pearls are damaged by perfume, hairspray, detergents, and perspiration. Apply perfumes or cosmetics before putting pearls on. Wipe with a damp cloth after wearing.
Coral	Perspiration will affect coral, dulling the color. Avoid all chemicals. Never soak. To clean, use a damp cloth.
Amber and ivory	Avoid contact with hairspray, perfumes, and cosmetics. To clean, wash in warm water with soap and wipe dry.
MINERAL GEMSTONES	
Diamond	Diamonds attract grease. Clean with a toothbrush in warm water and soap or dishwashing liquid, or in alcohol.
Opal	Opals may crack in freezing conditions and lose color in excessive heat. Never wash in hot water.
Turquoise	Liable to crack in extremes of temperature. Avoid contact with perfumes and cosmetics, which may cause stones to turn green. To clean, wipe with a damp cloth. Never soak.

MAKING JEWELRY

USE THE FOLLOWING step-by-step guide to make a pair of earrings and matching necklace. We have used multicolored tourmalines in this example, but you can substitute any stones of a similar size. If you are using gemstones of different colors, plan your pattern before you start in order to be certain that you have enough of each color.

TOURMALINE EARRINGS

EQUIPMENT

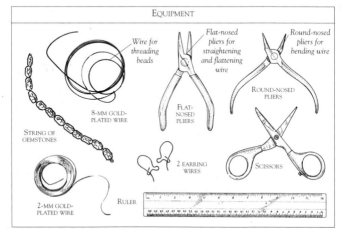

Wire for threading beads

Flat-nosed pliers for straightening and flattening wire

Round-nosed pliers for bending wire

8-MM GOLD-PLATED WIRE

FLAT-NOSED PLIERS

ROUND-NOSED PLIERS

STRING OF GEMSTONES

2 EARRING WIRES

SCISSORS

2-MM GOLD-PLATED WIRE

RULER

EARRINGS

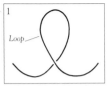

1 Cut a 2.3-in (6-cm) length of thick wire and bend it to form a loop.

Loop

Leave ends open

2 Make two small loops, leaving ends slightly open.

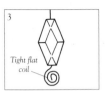

Tight flat coil

3 Cut three 2-in (5-cm) lengths of thin wire. Make tight flat coil at one end of piece of the thin wire and thread stone onto it.

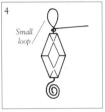

Small loop

4 Make small loop at other end and twist wire over itself to secure.

New loop

5 Trim excess wire to avoid sharp edges. Thread a new piece of thin wire through existing loop, and loop and twist wire again.

6 Thread another gemstone onto this wire, make loop, and secure as before. Repeat steps 5 and 6 to make V shape.

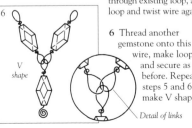

V shape

Detail of links

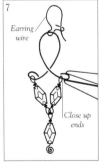

Earring wire

Close up ends

7 Secure the two stones on the thick wire and close up end loops with pliers. Place completed earring onto earring wire. Repeat whole process for second earring.

NECKLACE

1 Cut six 2.3-in (6-cm) lengths and twenty 1.2-in (3-cm) lengths of thick wire. Cut twelve 2-in (5-cm) lengths of thin wire.

2 Bend one 2.3-in strand of thick wire, as in earrings stages 1 and 2.

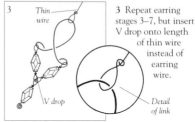

Thin wire

V drop

Detail of link

3 Repeat earring stages 3–7, but insert V drop onto length of thin wire instead of earring wire.

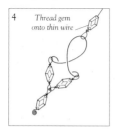

Thread gem onto thin wire

4 Loop and secure thin wire as before and thread gemstone onto it. Put to one side to use in stage 7.

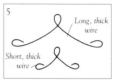

Long, thick wire

Short, thick wire

5 Bend four short, and five long, thick wires at center to form small loops and curl up ends.

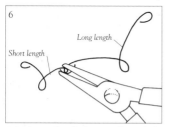

Long length

Short length

6 Link together the loops at the end of each short and long piece. Secure by closing the loops with pliers.

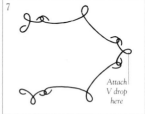

Attach V drop here

7 The long and short lengths should make an alternating pattern. Attach V drop to central link.

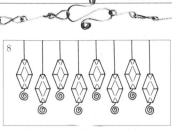

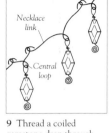

9

Necklace link

Central loop

8 With remaining eight lengths of thin wire, make coils as in earring stage 2 and thread a gemstone onto each strand.

9 Thread a coiled gemstone drop through the central loop of each necklace link. Secure as before and trim off any excess wire.

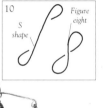

10

S shape

Figure eight

10 Bend eight 1.2-in (3-cm) lengths of thick wire into figure eights and eight into elongated S shapes.

Figure-eight link

S-shaped link

11 Join lengths together to make alternating pattern. Attach eight links to each side of necklace.

CLASP

1 Cut one 4.3-in (11-cm) and one 1.2-in (3-cm) length of thick wire.

Secure V drop to center of main necklace

2

2 Coil and bend longer wire into figure eight. Attach to necklace.

3

Clasp

Oval loop

3 Thread shorter wire onto other end of necklace and form oval loop large enough to hook clasp into it.

TABLE OF PROPERTIES

THIS TABLE SETS OUT the main features of each type
of gem, along with a rough guide to its value.
The gemstones are divided into eight categories,
depending on their structures (see pages 22-23).
Hardness is measured according to Mohs' scale,
which classifies minerals relative to each other on
a scale of 1 to 10 (see page 24). A gemstone's
specific gravity (SG) is its weight compared with
the weight of an equal volume of water (see page 25).
The "price" column indicates the comparative value
of each gem, calculated on the basis of an 0.3-in
(8-mm) diameter, cabochon-cut stone of average
quality. Where cabochon cuts do not apply, prices
for faceted gems are given. No specific figures are
listed, since gem prices are constantly fluctuating.

NAME	STRUCTURE	HARDNESS	SG	PRICE
Achroite (Tourmaline)	Trigonal	7.5	3.06	$$$
Agate (Chalcedony)	Amorphous	7	2.65	$
Almandine (Garnet)	Cubic	7.5	4.1	$
Amber	Amorphous	2.5	1.08	$
Amethyst (Quartz)	Trigonal	7	2.65	$
Aquamarine (Beryl)	Hexagonal	7.5	2.69	$$$
Azurite	Monoclinic	3.5	3.77	$
Bloodstone (Chalcedony)	Amorphous	7	2.65	$
Carnelian (Chalcedony)	Amorphous	7	2.65	$
Chalcedony	Amorphous	7	2.65	$
Chatoyant Quartz	Trigonal	7	2.65	$
Chrysoberyl	Orthorhombic	8.5	3.71	$$$$

NAME	STRUCTURE	HARDNESS	SG	PRICE
Chrysoprase (Chalcedony)	Amorphous	7	2.65	$
Citrine (Quartz)	Trigonal	7	2.65	$
Coral	Amorphous	3	2.68	$
Demantoid (Garnet)	Cubic	6.5	3.85	$$
Diamond	Cubic	10	3.52	$$$$
Dravite (Tourmaline)	Trigonal	7.5	3.06	$$
Emerald (Beryl)	Hexagonal	7.5	2.71	$$$$
Fire Agate (Chalcedony)	Amorphous	7	2.65	$$
Grossular (Garnet)	Cubic	7	3.49	$
Hauyne	Cubic	6	2.44	$$
Hessonite (Grossular Garnet)	Cubic	7.25	3.60	$
Ivory	Amorphous	2.5	1.90	N/A
Jadeite (Jade)	Amorphous	7	3.24	$
Jasper (Chalcedony)	Amorphous	7	2.65	$
Jet	Amorphous	2.5	1.33	$
Lapis Lazuli	Amorphous	5.5	2.80	$
Malachite	Monoclinic	4	4.00	$
Milky Quartz	Trigonal	7	2.65	$
Moonstone (Orthoclase)	Monoclinic	6	2.57	$
Nephrite (Jade)	Amorphous	6.5	2.96	$
Opal	Amorphous	6	2.10	$$
Orthoclase	Monoclinic	6	2.56	$
Padparadscha (Corundum)	Trigonal	9	4.00	$$$$
Pearl	Amorphous	3	2.71	$$$ *
Peridot	Orthorhombic	6.5	3.34	$$$
Pyrope (Garnet)	Cubic	7.25	3.80	$
Rock Crystal (Quartz)	Trigonal	7	2.65	$
Rose Quartz	Trigonal	7	2.65	$
Rubellite (Tourmaline)	Trigonal	7.5	3.06	$$$
Ruby (Corundum)	Trigonal	9	4.00	$$$$
Sapphire (Corundum)	Trigonal	9	4.00	$$$$
Sardonyx (Chalcedony)	Amorphous	7	2.65	$
Schorl (Tourmaline)	Trigonal	7.5	3.06	$$
Shell	Amorphous	2.5	1.30	$
Spessartine (Garnet)	Cubic	7	4.16	$$$
Spinel	Cubic	8	3.60	$$$
Topaz	Orthorhombic	8	3.54	$$
Turquoise	Amorphous	6	2.80	$
Uvarovite (Garnet)	Cubic	7.5	3.77	$$$$
Watermelon Tourmaline	Trigonal	7.5	3.06	$$
Zircon	Tetragonal	7.5	4.69	$$

(*price given is for 0.3-in (8-mm) cultured pearls)

Glossary

ALBITE
Important variety of feldspar; occurs in many types of rock.

ALLUVIAL DEPOSITS
Concentrations of fine-grained sediments that have been carried downstream and then deposited by rivers and streams.

ALUMINOUS SHALE
Shale is a rock made out of clay that has been buried and then compacted. The form known as aluminous shale contains traces of aluminum.

AMORPHOUS
Without regular internal atomic structure or external shape.

AMULET
Protective charm worn to ward off evil or illness, or to bring about good fortune.

ART DECO
Decorative style originating in Paris in the 1920s, marked by geometric motifs and well-defined outlines.

ART NOUVEAU
Late-19th-century style of art and architecture characterized by curved outlines often derived from nature.

BAGUETTE CUT
Rectangular step cut.

BASALT
Basalt rock forms at the Earth's surface and cools rapidly. It consists of small, poorly developed crystals.

BRILLIANT CUT
Most popular cut for diamonds and many other stones, especially colorless ones. It ensures that the maximum amount of light is reflected from the stone.

CABOCHON
A type of cut in which a gemstone has a domed upper surface.

CAMEO
Design in low relief, usually on a shell or type of agate, around which the background has been cut away.

CARAT
Standard measure of weight for precious stones. One carat equals 0.007 oz (0.2 g). The term is also used to describe the purity of gold. Pure gold is 24 carat.

CHATOYANCY
Cat's-eye effect shown by some stones when cut as a cabochon. Light is reflected along thin, iridescent bands.

CLEAVAGE
The way a mineral breaks along certain planes according to its internal structure.

CROWN
Top section of a cut stone, above the girdle.

CRYSTALLINE
Having a crystal structure.

CRYSTAL STRUCTURE
Internal atomic structure of crystals. Crystalline gems are classified according to seven basic structures.

DICHROIC
Gem that appears to be two different colors or shades when viewed from different directions.

DIFFRACTION
The splitting of white light into its constituent colors.

DOUBLET
Composite stone made of two pieces cemented or glued together.

EROSION
The transportation of material from its original site by weathering – processes involving wind, water, and ice.

FACET
One surface of a cut gemstone.

FACETING
The cutting and polishing of the surfaces of a gemstone into facets. The style of cut is dependent on the number and shape of the facets.

FANCY
Diamond of an unusual natural color.

FANCY CUT
Name given to a stone with an unconventional shape when cut.

FIRE
Term used for dispersed light. A gem with strong fire is unusually bright.

GIRDLE
Band around the widest part of a cut stone, where the crown meets the pavilion.

GRANITE
Coarse-grained igneous rock.

HEAT-TREATMENT
Application of heat to a gem aimed at enhancing its color or clarity.

IGNEOUS ROCK
Rock that has formed from erupted volcanic lava or solidified magma.

INCLUSION
Solid, liquid, or gaseous particle contained within a mineral. Often adds interest to a stone.

INTAGLIO
Design in which the subject is cut lower than the background. Often used for signet rings.

INTERGROWN
When two or more minerals grow together and become interlocked.

IRIDESCENCE
Reflection of light caused by internal features of a gem, giving rise to a rainbowlike play of colors.

LAVA
Molten rock, erupted from volcanoes.

LUSTER
The intensity of light reflected off a gem's surface.

MAGMA
Rock in a molten state below the Earth's surface.

MANTLE
Layer of the Earth between the core and the crust. It is about 1,740 miles (2,900 km) thick.

MATRIX
The rock in which a gem is found.

METAMORPHIC ROCK
Type of rock that forms from other rocks owing to the action of heat and pressure, or heat alone.

MICROCRYSTALLINE
Mineral structure in which crystals are too small to be seen with the naked eye.

MIXED CUT
Cut in which the facets above and below the girdle are styled in different ways, usually brilliant cut above and step cut below.

MOHS' SCALE
Measure of a mineral's hardness in relation to other minerals, on a scale of 1 to 10.

OILING
Process of applying mineral oil to certain stones, mainly emeralds, to mask their inclusions; turn the stones a darker, more favorable hue; and make them more transparent.

OPALESCENCE
Milky blue form of iridescence.

OPAQUE
Exhibiting opacity, blocking the passage of light.

PAVILION
Lower part of stone, below the girdle.

PEGMATITE
Igneous rock, which forms as the liquids from magma cool. It consists of unusually large crystals.

PENDELOQUE CUT
Lozenge-shaped, fancy cut, often used for flawed gems.

POROUS
Containing pores, or holes, that allow a substance to be penetrated by water, other fluids, or air.

RESIN
Sticky substance obtained from certain plants.

RIVER GRAVEL
Deposit of minerals that have been broken down and washed downstream, occasionally containing gemstones.

ROUGH
Term used to describe a rock or crystal still in its natural state, before cutting or polishing.

SEDIMENTARY ROCK
Type of rock at the Earth's surface. It consists of layers of rock fragments or other substances that have been deposited on top of one another and have hardened.

SILICA
Hard, glossy mineral usually occurring as quartz. Silica is the main constituent of sandstone.

SPECIFIC GRAVITY
The comparison of a mineral's weight with the weight of an equal volume of water.

SPECTROSCOPE
Instrument used to identify different gemstones. It reveals the bands of light

that a gemstone absorbs.

STEP CUT
Rectangular- or square-shaped cut with several facets parallel to the edges of the stone. It is generally used for colored stones.

STRIATIONS
Parallel scratches, grooves, or lines in a mineral.

SYNTHETIC GEMSTONE
Laboratory-made stone whose chemical composition and optical properties are similar to those of its natural equivalent.

TALISMAN
Good-luck charm believed to possess magical powers.

TRANSLUCENT
Permitting the passage of, but diffusing, light.

TRANSPARENT
Permitting the passage of light without diffusion.

VITREOUS
Glasslike quality (used to describe a gem's luster).

WEATHERING
The breaking down of rocks by the action of various processes, such as freezing, thawing, and dissolving in water.

Resources

MUSEUMS

American Museum of Natural History
Central Park West
at 79th Street
New York, NY 10024
The collection includes
exhibits of cut, uncut, and
carved examples of both
precious and semiprecious
gemstones, including the
Star of India – the largest
star sapphire in the world.

Cleveland Museum of Natural History
1 Wade Oval Drive
University Circle
Cleveland, OH 44106
Among the gems on
exhibit are colored
diamonds, opals, and
mineral eggs and
cabochons.

Field Museum of Natural History
1400 South Lake Shore
Drive
Chicago, IL 60605
This museum has both a
gem room, with precious
stones, and a jade room.

National Museum of Natural History
10th Street and
Constitution Avenue NW
Smithsonian Institution
Washington, DC 20560
The founder of the
Smithsonian was a
mineralogist whose 10,000
specimens formed the
basis for the National
Mineral Collection and
the National Gem
Collection. The highlight
of the collection is the
Hope Diamond, a blue
diamond made into a
pendant.

Natural History Museum of Los Angeles County
900 Exposition Boulevard
Los Angeles, CA 90007
In addition to an exhibit
on gemstone formation
and specimens that can
be touched, including a
several-hundred-pound
block of jadeite, the
collection has uncut
emeralds, aquamarines,
and tourmalines; an
18-carat star ruby; and
a 4,644-carat topaz.

ORGANIZATIONS

Gemological Institute of America
The Robert Mouawad
Campus
5345 Armada Drive
Carlsbad, CA 92008

International Colored Gemstones Association
19 W. 21st Street
New York, NY 10010

International Gemological Institute
589 Fifth Avenue
New York, NY 10017

Index

A
achroite, 70
  color key, 39
adamantine luster, 27
agate, 12, 13, 78, 79
  color key, 45
  fire agate, 47, 119
  formation, 21
  moss agate, 43
Albert, Prince Consort, 101
Alexander II, tsar, 59
alexandrite, 58, 59
Alfonso XII, king of Spain, 111
almandine, 73
  color key, 40
amber, 33, 104–5
  care and cleaning, 113
  color key, 43
  luster, 27
amethyst, 76–7
  color key, 46
  formation, 21
amorphous structure, 22
aquamarine, 66–7
  color key, 46
  crystal structure, 23
  distribution, 18–19
  formation, 20
Art Deco, 59, 65, 86
Art Nouveau, 85
artificial gems, 17, 34–5
Australia, 30
axes of symmetry, 23

axinite, 43
Ayurvedic medicine, 14
azurite, 92
  color key, 46
  crystal structure, 23
  formation, 21

B
Balas rubies, 61
baroque pearls, 97
birthstones, 15
black coral, 99
black gems, 47
bloodstone, 78
  color key, 44
blue gemstones, 46
Braganza Diamond, 110
Brazilian Princess, 62
British Imperial State Crown,
  60–1
Burton, Richard, 52

C
cabochons, 16, 28
cameos, 106
cannel coal, 47
carats, 24, 25
carbon, 52
care of gems, 112–13
carnelian, 12, 13, 78, 79
  color key, 42
Cartier, 67, 91, 111
cassiterite, 42

Castiglione, countess of, 111
cat's-eye, 58, 59, 110–11
  color key, 43
celestine, 39
cerussite, 39
chalcedony, 78–9
Charles II, king of England, 110
Chatham, Carroll, 64
chatoyancy, 79
chatoyant quartz, 43, 118
China, 12
Chinese medicine, 14
chrysoberyl, 58–9
  color key, 43
  distribution, 18–19
  formation, 20
chrysoprase, 78, 79
  color key, 44
  crystal structure, 22
citrine, 74, 75, 76
  color key, 42
  formation, 21
clasps, 117
cleaning gemstones, 113
cleavage, 22
Cleopatra, 97
color, 26–7
color key, 37–47
colorless gems, 39
conch shells, 106
conchiolin, 99
Cook Islands, 12
coral, 32, 98–9

care and cleaning, 113
color key, 41, 47
harvesting, 19
corundum, 54
Crown Jewels, 110
crystal balls, 14, 75
crystals:
  growing, 34
  structure, 22–3
cubic gems, 23
cubic zirconia, 39
Cullinan Diamond, 52
cultured pearls, 96–7
cuts, 28–9
cymophane see cat's-eye

D
danburite, 39
demantoid, 44, 119
density, 25
diamond, 12, 50–3
  care and cleaning, 113
  color key, 45, 47
  distribution, 18–19
  formation, 20
  luster, 27
  mining, 31
  panning for, 18
donkey's-ear abalone, 41
doublets, garnet-topped, 35, 45
dravite, 42, 119
Dresden Green, 52

E
earrings, making, 115
Edward, Black Prince, 61

Edward VII, king of England, 52, 82
Egypt, 12, 14, 90
Elizabeth, the Queen Mother, 53
emerald, 64–5
  color key, 44
  distribution, 18–19
  formation, 20
  synthetic gems, 35
equipment, jewelry making, 114
euclase, 45

F
Fabergé, Carl, 85
Fersen, count Axel de, 110–11
fire agate, 47, 119
fire opal, 42, 87
flame-fusion technique, 34
fluorite, 45
flux-melt technique, 17, 35
Frémy, Edmond, 17

G
Gahn, J. G., 61
gahnospinel, 61
garnet, 72–3
  color key, 40, 45
  distribution, 18–19
  formation, 20, 21
  garnet-topped doublets, 35, 45
Gilson, Pierre, 35, 90
glass, 39, 100
  color key, 47
Great Star of Africa, 52
green gemstones, 44–5
grossular garnet:

color key, 40, 45
physical properties, 119
growing crystals, 34
Gustavus III, king of Sweden, 70

H
hardness, 24–5
hauyne, 46, 119
healing, 14–15, 75
heliodor, 42
hessonite, 42, 119
hexagonal gems, 23
Hildegard, St, 63
history of gemstones, 12–13
Hope Diamond, 53

I
identifying gems, 26, 35
idiochromatic gems, 27
imperial jade, 80
inclusions, 24
indicolite, 70
iridescent gemstones, 47
ivory, 33, 102–3
  care and cleaning, 113
  color key, 41

J
jade, 12, 80–1
jadeite, 80–1
  color key, 41, 44
  formation, 20
Japan, 32
jasper, 78, 119
jet, 32, 100–1
  color key, 47
  crystal structure, 22
jewelry, making, 114–17

K
Knoop hardness scale, 25
Koh-i-noor Diamond, 53
kyanite, 45

L
lapis lazuli, 12, 90–1
  color key, 46
  colors, 27
  formation, 21
  medicinal uses, 14
lazurite, 90
legendary gems, 110–11
leopard claws, 15
Lippert, Felice, 111
Louis XVI, king of France,
  53
loupe, 35
luster, 26–7

M
making jewelry, 114–17
malachite, 92–3
  color key, 44
  formation, 21
  luster, 27
Marie Antoinette, queen
  of France, 110–11
medicine, 14–15
milky quartz, 41, 119
mineral gemstones, 16, 49–93
mining, 30–1
Mohs, Friedrich, 24
Mohs' hardness scale, 24–5
monoclinic gems, 23
moonstone, 84–5
  color key, 39
  formation, 20

moss agate, 43
mother-of-pearl, 47, 106, 107
mourning jewelry, 100
Myanmar (Burma), 31
myths, 14–15

N
nacre, 96
Namibia, 31
natural pearls, 96
necklaces, making, 116–17
nephrite, 80–1
  color key, 41, 44
Nigeria, 15
Noah, 72
North American Indians, 15

O
olivine, 83
onyx, 100
opal, 86–7
  care and cleaning, 113
  color key, 47
  distribution, 18–19
  fire opal, 42, 87
  formation, 21
  mining, 30
  synthetic gems, 35
organic gemstones, 17, 32–3,
  95–107
orthoclase:
  color key, 39, 43
orthorhombic gems, 23

P
padparadscha, 42, 119
paint pigments, 38
panning, 30–1

particolored gems, 27
paua shell, 45, 107
pearls, 17, 32, 96–7
  care and cleaning, 113
  color key, 41, 47
  distribution, 18–19
  diving for, 19
  medicinal uses, 14
Pedro the Cruel, king
  of Spain, 61
peridot, 82–3
  color key, 44
  distribution, 18–19
  formation, 20
  physical properties, 24–5,
  18–19
Pliny, 97, 101
Poland, 15
polishing, 28–9
pyrope, 72
  color key, 40

Q
quartz, 74–5
  chalcedony, 78–9
  chatoyant quartz, 43, 118
  crystal structure, 23
  formation, 20
  milky quartz, 41, 119
  rose quartz, 74, 75, 119
  smoky quartz, 42

R
red gemstones, 40–1
resinous lustre, 27
rock crystal, 74, 76
  color key, 39
  crystal balls, 14, 75

Romans, 13
rose quartz, 74, 75
rubber, vulcanized, 47, 100
rubellite, 70
  color key, 40
ruby, 12, 54–5
  color key, 40
  cuts, 16
  distribution, 18–19
  formation, 16, 20, 21
  imitation gems, 35
  mining, 30
  synthetic, 17
ruby spinel, 61
Ruser, William, 77

S
Sancy Diamond, 53
sapphire, 12, 56–7
  color key, 39, 40, 43, 45, 46
  distribution, 18–19
  formation, 20, 21
sardonyx, 78
  color key, 42
scarab charms, 12
scheelite, 39
schorl, 71
  color key, 47
seed pearls, 96
shell, 12, 106–7
  color key, 41
silver-colored gems, 41
Smithsonite, 45
smoky quartz, 42
South Africa, 31, 52
specific gravity, 24, 25
spectroscope, 26

spessartine, 73
  color key, 40, 43
  formation, 20, 21
spinel, 60–1
  color key, 41, 46
  crystal structure, 23
  formation, 20, 21
staurolite, 43
stone fetishes, 15
storage, 112
strontium titanate, 39
sunstone, 42
symmetry, axes of, 23
synthetic gems, 17, 34–5

T
Taylor, Elizabeth, 52
tetragonal gems, 23
Tibet, 13
Tiffany & Co., 53, 91, 111
Tiffany Diamond, 53
tiger's-eye, 79
titanite, 43
topaz, 62–3
  color key, 40, 46
  crystal structure, 23
  distribution, 18–19
  formation, 20
tortoiseshell, 33, 106
  color key, 47
tourmaline, 70–1
  color key, 40, 45
  colors, 27
  distribution, 18–19
  formation, 20
triclinic gems, 23
trigonal gems, 23
turquoise, 12, 88–9

care and cleaning, 113
  color key, 46
  crystal structure, 23
  formation, 21
  Tibetan jewellery, 13

U
uvarovite, 44, 119

V
verdelite, 71
Verneuil, August, 34
Verneuil method, 17, 34
vesuvianite, 43
Victoria, queen of England, 53, 101
violet gemstones, 46
vitreous lustre, 27
vulcanite, 47, 100

W
watermelon tourmaline, 71
  color key, 40, 45
Whitby jet, 100, 101
white coral, 99
white gemstones, 41
Windsor, Duchess of, 111

Y
yellow–brown gems 42–3

Z
zircon, 68–9
  color key, 39, 45
  crystal structure, 23
  formation, 21

Acknowledgments

Dorling Kindersley would like to thank:
Stephen Bradshaw of the jeweler Pearl Cross Ltd. for the generous loan of his jewelry; Emma Foa for her handmade jewelry; Carole Oliver for the loan of her personal jewelry; Dennis Durham, gem cutter, for his expert knowledge and patience; Fiona Gamble of the jeweler Bentley & Co. for her unstinting enthusiasm; David Mayor for his research into traditional medicine; Hilary Bird for the index; Tanya Tween, Robin Hunter, Earl Neish, and Jacqui Burton, for design assistance; Caroline Potts for picture library services.

Photographs by:
Steve Gorton. Additional photography by Ken Findlay, Colin Keates, Harry Taylor, Mathew Ward.

Illustrations by:
Sarah Ponder, Aziz Khan, Janet Allis, John Hutchinson, Peter Visscher, Caroline Church, Janos Marffy, Alistair Wardle.

Picture Credits:
c = center; b = bottom; l = left; r = right; t = top
The publisher would like to thank the following for their kind permission to reproduce their photographs:
The Ancient Art and Architecture Collection Ltd: 14tr; **Amber Centre:** 105bl; **Courtesy of Argos:** 69tr; **Bentley and Co:** 4c, 4cr, 5cl, 5cr, 7tc, 17bl, 50bc, 50br, 51crb, 54cl, 55cl, 57cla, 59cr, 62tr, 63tr, 64cla, 64bc, 65tr, 66tl, 67crb, 67cbl, 72cla, 73cl, 73br, 85bc, 86clb, 87br, 88–89, 89bc, 98cr;

Bridgeman Art Library: Cheltenham Art Gallery and Museums, Gloucester: Hair comb by Fred Partridge 85tr; Christie's Images 60cl; Giraudon 12bl; Private Collection 101bl; **Bruce Coleman Ltd:** Gerald Cubitt 18cl; Charles and Sandra Hood 19cb; John Murray 32cb; **Christie's Images:** 3c, 35br, 51t, 51br, 59bl, 62bc, 70bl, 71bl, 74clb, 76tl, 77tr, 77bl, 78cla, 80tl, 80cr, 81cl, 81tr, 81bl, 81br, 82tl, 83bl, 87tc, 91tr, 91bc, 94–95, 98cl; **Crown Copyright. Historic Royal Palaces:** 52br, 61cl; **De Beers:** 28tr, 29tr, 31br, 31cla, 52tr, 53cl, 53tl, 53tr, 110br; **Eye Ubiquitous:** 32tl; **Michael Freeman:** 19tl, 30cla, 48–49; **Robert Harding Picture Library:** 13br; **Michael Holford:** 101tl; **Hulton Getty:** 53br, 111bl; **The Natural History Museum, London:** 16–17, 16cl, 21crb, 24–25, 26br, 28bc, 30bl, 34tr, 34br, 34bc, 35c, 35cbl, 38cl, 51cr, 104tl; **Rex Features:** 52bl; **Science Photo Library:** Peter Menzel 30br; David Parker 26tr; **Sotheby's Picture Library:** 55tr, 76bl, 85bl; **Smithsonian Institute:** 62br, 66cla; **By Courtesy of the Board of Trustees of the Victoria and Albert Museum:** 97tr; **The Worshipful Company of Goldsmiths:** 79bl.

Every effort has been made to trace the copyright holders and we apologize in advance for any unintentional omissions. We would be pleased to insert appropriate acknowledgment in any subsequent edition of this publication.

All other images © Dorling Kindersley
For further information see:
www.dkimages.com